CORNER-TO-CORNER
BLANKETS TO CROCHET

A QUARTO BOOK

This edition published in 2024 by
Search Press
Wellwood
North Farm Road
Tunbridge Wells
Kent TN2 3DR

ISBN: 978-1-80092-265-5
ebook ISBN: 978-1-80093-264-7

Conceived, edited and designed by
Quarto Publishing, an imprint of
The Quarto Group
1 Triptych Place
London SE1 9SH
www.quarto.com

QUAR.1173852

Assistant editor: Ella Whiting
Copyeditor: May Corfield
Pattern checker: Juliette Watson
Cover and layout designer: Sally Bond
Designer: Eliana Holder
Art director: Martina Calvio
Photographer: Leanne Jade
Stylist: Claire Montgomerie
Publisher: Lorraine Dickey

Printed in China

Bookmarked Hub
For further ideas and inspiration, and to join our free
online community, visit www.bookmarkedhub.com

CORNER-TO-CORNER
BLANKETS TO CROCHET

Leonie Morgan

Search Press

Contents

Beginner designs

Intermediate designs

Advanced designs

Chapter 3: PROJECTS 116

About This Book

With this colourful guide, you'll learn how to crochet 18 blankets and two fabulous projects for your home. Master the basics of corner-to-corner crochet with an opening chapter that outlines all the tools, materials, and techniques you'll need, then put your crochet skills to the test as you make the throws and homeware projects that comprise the heart of this book.

Organized by skill level, beginning with the easier designs and working through intermediate and advanced ones, the book's intuitive structure allows you to start with the project you feel most drawn to, no matter your experience.

THE BLANKET PATTERNS (PAGES 26–113)

At the heart of this book are the 18 blanket designs, including the Copenhagen throw shown below. Each includes a written pattern, colour charts, and photographs of the finished throw that will help you start crocheting right away.

Each project features a panel that outlines the basics at a glance, including a skill level indicator and information on hook size, block stitches, and throw size. Some designs also list individual square size and the specific techniques you'll need to crochet the throw.

A list of relevant abbreviations and stitches is included for each pattern.

The patterns in this book use Cascade Yarns®, with the specific type, names, and colour codes listed here referring specifically to this yarn. You can follow this list exactly for each pattern or make comparable substitutions if you prefer.

Full-colour charts and photographs provide visual references for the completed design.

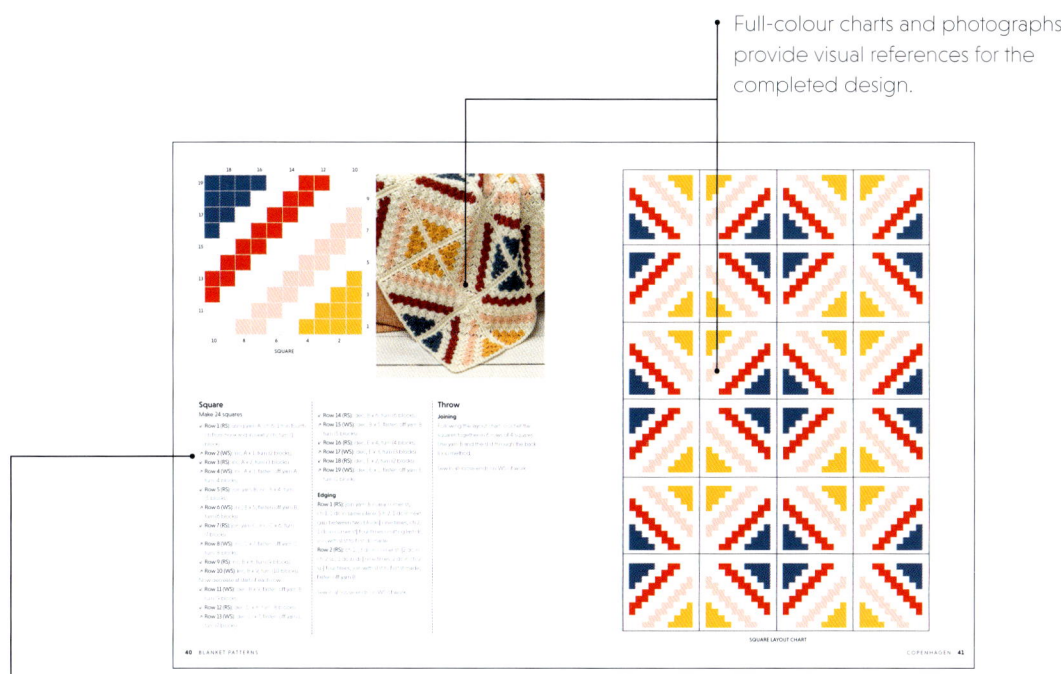

A written pattern takes you through the design, row by row. Where relevant, instructions for making squares or strips, or for edging and joining, are also included.

TECHNIQUES (PAGES 12–25)

This section provides information on the tools and materials required, the crochet stitches and techniques you'll need, and how to read crochet charts.

Written instructions are broken down into small, easy-to-understand steps.

Photos help make written instructions even clearer for beginner crocheters.

Meet Leonie

My name is Leonie, and I'm a crochet designer, knitter, cross-stitcher, photographer, and general crafty soul. I live in Wales, UK, in a valley with a long history of wool-making, so I feel right at home with wool projects, and I love the historical links to yarn right on my doorstep. If I'm not home crocheting (with Hubble the cat assisting with yarn management), I'll be out in the wild woods with my camera and a head full of folk tales, or up on the hills enjoying the peace.

I'm a crochet addict with a large yarn stash and more crochet throws than I'll ever need! I will never admit to the number of works in progress I have. Neither will I officially admit to how I keep buying yarns for 'something' and now have no space to store them. Sound familiar? Well, I hope this book will help you make a dent in your yarn stash – or encourage a trip to your local yarn shop!

I am drawn to designing with aran (worsted)- or DK (light worsted)-weight yarn and love playing with colour. I enjoy coming up with new block patterns and new row-by-row patterns and just wish there was more time in the day to design. Whatever I'm designing, the colour choice is the most exciting bit. The process of designing, from initial fumbling with scrap yarn to picking colours and writing up patterns, is a ton of fun. And the best bit? Sharing my designs with you!

I'm delighted to have finished this corner-to-corner crochet book, and I hope it will inspire you to grab your hook and get crocheting. What a big project it was! I haven't downed hooks yet though, so if you'd like to know more about my crochet journey, you can browse my latest designs, get inspired, and keep up to date with me at www.leoniemorgan.com and @woolnhook on Instagram.

Happy hooking!
Leonie

chapter 1

TECHNIQUES

Materials, Hooks and Yarns

When you walk into a yarn shop, you'll find endless yarns in bright and bold colours, differing weights, and all types of textures. The choice is exciting but can be a little daunting, and the same is true for hooks and accessories. Use this guide to find out what you need to get started.

CROCHET HOOKS

Hooks come in different sizes and materials. The material a hook is made from can affect your tension. When starting out, it's best to use aluminium hooks, as they have a pointed head, well-defined throat, and work well with most yarns. Bamboo hooks are also pleasing to work with but can be slippery with some yarns.

Plastic hooks can be squeaky with synthetic yarns. You can also purchase hooks with soft grip or wooden handles, which are great to work with.

What size hook?

You may find that using the hook size recommended for a particular yarn or pattern isn't satisfactory, and your work may be too tight or too loose. Try different hook sizes until you are happy. Ultimately, you want to use a hook and yarn weight that you are comfortable with – yarn/hook recommendations are not set in stone. Be aware that not all yarn labels give a recommended hook size. Use the recommended knitting needle size as a guide, or use a hook one or two sizes bigger.

OTHER TOOLS

Although all you need to get started is a hook and some yarn, it's handy to have the following items in your bag.

Scissors

Always use a pair of small, sharp embroidery scissors.

Ruler and measuring tape

A rigid ruler is best for measuring tension. A sturdy measuring tape is good for taking larger measurements.

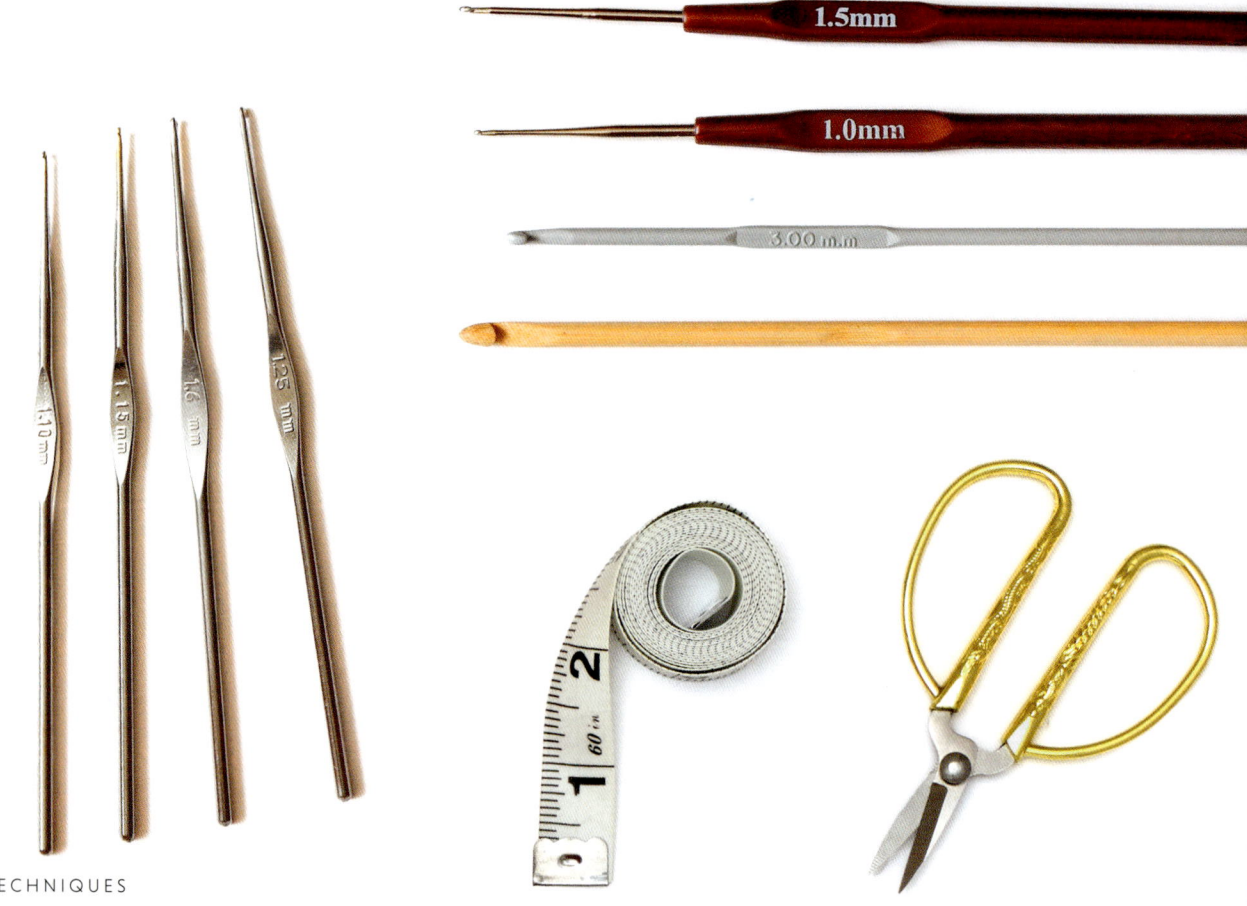

Stitch markers

Split-ring markers are handy for keeping track of the first stitch of a row or round, particularly when starting out. Also use them to hold the working loop when you put your work down.

Pins

Use rustproof, glass-head pins for blocking.

Needles

Yarn or tapestry needles are used for sewing seams and sewing in yarn ends. Choose needles with blunt ends to avoid splitting stitches. Yarn needles have different-sized eyes, so choose one that will accommodate the weight of yarn you will be using.

YARN CHOICE

Suitable yarns for crochet range from very fine cotton to bulky wool. As a general rule, yarns that have a smooth texture and a medium or high twist are the easiest to work with. I chose to crochet with Cascade Yarns® Cascade 220® and Cascade 220 Superwash® for many of the patterns in this book because it comes in a huge variety of colours, is easy to work with, and is machine-washable. If you use a different yarn weight or brand, it's a good idea to buy just one ball before you purchase enough yarn to complete a project. Make a test swatch, wash it following the instructions on the ball band, block it to shape, and think about whether you were comfortable using the yarn and if it turned out how you'd intended.

YARN FIBRES

Yarns come in a range of different fibres and combinations.

Wool

Wool is a resilient fibre that feels good to crochet with and has great stitch definition. Do find out whether or not the wool can be machine-washed.

Acrylic

Acrylic yarn is an affordable choice for beginners and popular with crochet enthusiasts. It's great for practising stitches and techniques and testing colour combinations. Although acrylic can pill and lose its shape eventually, it has the benefit of being machine-washable, making it a good choice for items that may require frequent washing.

Wool/synthetic mixes

A yarn composed of both wool and synthetic fibre is a dependable choice. Picking something that has a small percentage of synthetic fibre (for example, nylon or acrylic) makes a nice yarn to work with and launder, while still retaining the advantages of wool.

Cotton and cotton mixes

Cotton can present more of a challenge for beginners. It can be a little stiff to work with, but the stitches are crisp and neat. A cotton mix is usually softer to

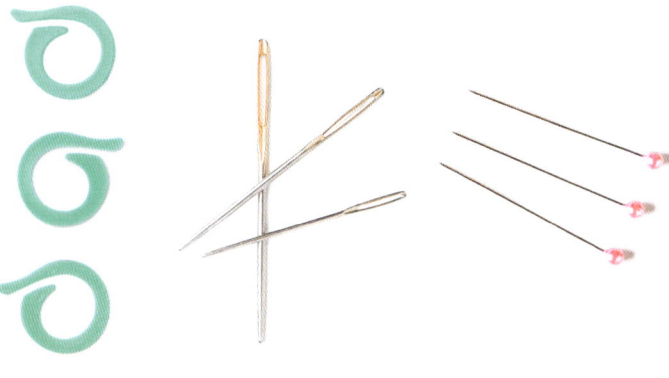

Starting and Finishing

Here's how to get started on your project. All the patterns and projects in this book begin with a foundation chain.

HOLDING THE HOOK AND YARN

The most common way of holding the hook is shown here, but if this doesn't feel comfortable to you, try grasping the flat section of the hook between your thumb and forefinger as if you were holding a pen.

1 Holding the hook like a knife is the most widely used method. Centre the tips of your right thumb and forefinger over the flat section of the hook.

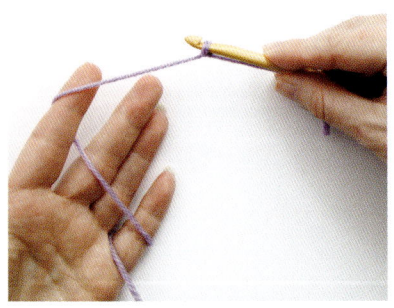

2 To control the supply and keep an even tension on the yarn, loop the short end of the yarn over your left forefinger, and take the yarn coming from the ball loosely around the little finger on the same hand. Use the middle finger and thumb to help hold the work. If you are left-handed, hold the hook in your left hand and the yarn in your right.

MAKING A SLIP KNOT

1 Loop the yarn as shown, insert the hook into the loop, catch the yarn with the hook, and pull it through to make a loop over the hook.

2 Gently pull the yarn to tighten the loop around the hook and complete the slip knot.

FOUNDATION CHAIN

The pattern will tell you how many chains to make. This may be a specific number or a multiple. If a pattern tells you to make a multiple of 3 + 2, this does not mean make a multiple of 5. It means that you should make a multiple of 3 and then add 2 chains – for example, 3 + 2, 6 + 2, 9 + 2, and so on. You may also be instructed to add a turning chain for the first row.

1 Holding the hook in your right hand and the yarn in your left, pinch the yarn tail beneath the slip knot between your thumb and middle finger of your left hand, then wrap the yarn round the hook. Draw the yarn through to make a new loop and complete the first chain stitch.

2 Repeat this process, drawing a new loop of yarn through the loop already on the hook until the foundation chain is the required length. Count each V-shaped loop on the front of the chain as one chain stitch, except for the loop on the hook, which is not counted. After every few stitches, move up the thumb and finger that are grasping the chain to keep the chain stitches even.

Basic Stitches

All crochet stitches are based on a loop pulled through another loop by a hook. There are only a few stitches to master, each of a different length. Here is a guide to the basic stitches used in this book.

FASTENING OFF

When you have completed your crochet, cut the yarn about 15cm (6in) from the last stitch. Wrap the yarn round the hook and draw the yarn end through the loop on the hook. Gently pull the yarn to tighten the last stitch, then sew in the yarn end.

SEWING IN ENDS

For crochet worked in rows, use a yarn needle to sew in ends diagonally on the wrong side. For crochet worked in rounds, sew in ends under stitches for 2.5cm (1in) or so. If the pattern doesn't allow this, sew under a few stitches, then up through the back of a stitch and under a few stitches on the next row.

CHAIN (CH)

Wrap the yarn round the hook and pull it through the loop on the hook to form a new loop on the hook.

SLIP STITCH (SL ST)

Insert the hook into the specified stitch, wrap the yarn round, and pull it through the stitch and the loop on the hook.

DOUBLE CROCHET (DC)

Insert the hook into the specified stitch, wrap the yarn round, and pull it through the stitch (2 loops on hook). Yarn round and pull it through both loops.

TREBLE CROCHET (TR)

Yarn round, insert the hook into the specified stitch, yarn round, and pull it through the stitch (3 loops on hook). *Yarn round and pull it through two loops; repeat from * once more.

NOTE ON ABBREVIATIONS

The patterns in this book use UK crochet terms. Crochet stitches are worked in the same way in both the UK and US, but the stitch names are not the same and identical names are used for different stitches. See below for UK terms and the US equivalent.

UK	US
Double crochet (dc)	Single crochet (sc)
Treble crochet (tr)	Double crochet (dc)
Half treble crochet (htr)	Half double (hdc)

Diagonal Box Stitch

Corner-to-corner crochet uses the diagonal box stitch to create blocks (also called tiles). The diagonal box stitch can be made using treble crochet or half treble crochet, but throughout this book, we'll only be using treble crochet stitches to create each block.

FIRST ROW

To work the first block of the project, start with a sl st on your hook.

1 Ch 6.

a

b

2 In the 4th ch from your hook, work 1 tr, work 1 tr in each of the next 2 ch. You can work into any of the loops of the chain stitches. I prefer to work into the bump at the back of the chain but you can choose otherwise. Just remember to stick with whichever loop you choose for a neat look.

SECOND ROW

1 Ch 6.

2 1 tr in 4th ch from hook and into the next 2 ch.

a

b

a

b

3 Flip the first block you made upward, and work a sl st into the 3-ch sp.

4 Ch 3, 3 tr into 3-ch sp.

Step 4 is the block stitch used throughout the book on all projects.

Decreases

a

a

c

b

b

To make a decrease at the start of a row (a), you begin by working a sl st in each of the next 3 stitches and into the next ch sp (b). Then ch 3 to continue (c).

To make a decrease at the end of a row, you just omit working a block in the last ch sp. It's important to work a sl st into that missed ch sp to secure the row.

JOIN-AS-YOU-GO

a

b

1. Join yarn and ch 3.

2. Sl st into space between blocks (you may have to turn here depending on where you are starting).

3. Ch 3.
Turn and work a block as normal.

JOIN THE LAST BLOCK OF A ROW

a

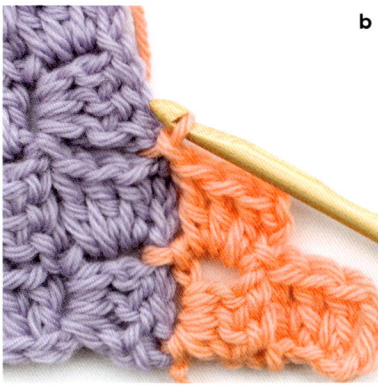

b

After working the last block, join by working a sl st between blocks of the piece you are joining to.

Ch 3 and sl st in the next space between blocks.

Turn and work the first block of the next row. Continue in this way until the pieces are completely joined.

Colourwork

Many patterns use a single colour for each row or round, with a new colour being joined at the end of a row or round. In some patterns you'll need to change colours along a row multiple times.

COLOUR CHANGES

When the pattern indicates that it's time to create a block in a new colour, you will actually begin the colour change in the last yarn round hook of the original-coloured block.

To do this, you will pick up the new yarn when working the last stitch of a block by picking up the new colour and pulling it through the last 2 loops of your third treble crochet.

When changing colours at the beginning of a row, you'll do something very similar, depending on if you're working an increase or decrease block.

When beginning an increase row in a new colour, the colour change will take place in the final yarn round hook of the previous row. Chain 6 with the new colour and proceed as usual.

For a decrease row, you will fasten off the previous colour at the end of the last row, turn your work, and then attach or pick up the new colour in the last ch sp made. Continue working blocks as normal.

CHANGING COLOUR MID-ROW

When working the last stitch of the old colour, omit the final stage (the last yarn round hook) to leave the stitch incomplete. Wrap the new yarn round, and draw it through all of the loops on the hook to complete the stitch. The new yarn will form the top loops of the next stitch in the new colour. If the pattern states to fasten off the previous colour, snip the yarn, leaving approximately 15cm (6in) and leave on the wrong side of your work. After you've worked a couple of rows, you can then sew in the loose end neatly.

WORKING OVER UNUSED COLOURS

When working over an unused colour, hold the carried thread to the back of your work and crochet over it. When carrying more than one colour, hold the colour with the most contrast to the working yarn at the back and the yarn with the least contrast toward the front while keeping both strands at the back of the work.

YARN MANAGEMENT

When working with a number of colours, things can get a bit messy very quickly. Keeping bobbins or entire hanks of a colour attached helps minimize the ends to weave in. However, the yarn can get a bit tangled, so here are some tips to help:

- **Very Important:** always leave your unused yarns and snipped ends on the wrong side of your work.
- Wind yarn onto small clips to create a bobbin. You can clip the bobbins to the back of the project when the colour is not in use. Other kinds of bobbins work equally well too. I tend to wind approximately 10m (11yd) of yarn onto the bobbins so that they aren't too heavy but, if you make sure your stitches aren't pulled too taut by the weight, you can wind as much onto your bobbins as you need.
- Flip your work consistently. If you turn your work from left to right at the end of one row, turn it back from right to left on the next row.
- Untangle as you go. It's bound to happen, so take a couple of moments to straighten out your yarn every few rows or at the end of a session of crocheting. If things get very tangled, you can always cut the yarn and reattach it to your project.

Tension and Blocking

It's important to crochet a test swatch before you start your project to establish tension. To finish off a block neatly, you will need to block it. You can use the tension swatch to test blocking and laundering methods.

TENSION

The tension throughout this book differs depending on the yarn recommended. Here is the tension you'll need to match:

Cascade 220 Superwash® (DK) and 5mm (US H-8) hook: 6 blocks x 6 blocks = 10cm (4in)

Cascade 220® (aran) and 6mm (US J-10) hook: 5 blocks x 5 blocks = 10cm (4in)

Cascade Magnum (super chunky) and 12mm (US O-16) hook: 2 blocks x 2 blocks = 10cm (4in)

MEASURING TENSION

No two people will crochet to the same tension, even when working with identical yarn and hooks. Always make a test swatch or block before starting a project so that you can compare your tension with the pattern tension and get an idea of how the finished project will feel and drape. It's also useful for testing out different colour combinations.

To test your tension, make a sample swatch or block in the yarn you intend to use following the pattern directions. Block the sample and then measure again. If your sample is larger, try making another using a smaller hook. If your sample is smaller, try making another using a bigger hook. Also do this if the fabric feels too loose and floppy or too dense and rigid. Keep trying until you find a hook size that will give you the required tension, or until you are happy with the drape and feel of your work. Ultimately, it's more important that you use a hook and yarn you are comfortable with than that you rigidly follow the pattern instructions.

BLOCKING

Blocking is crucial to set the stitches and even out the piece. Choose a method based on the care label of the yarn. When in doubt, use the wet method. Use an ironing board or old quilt, or make a blocking board by securing one or two layers of quilter's wadding, covered with a sheet of cotton fabric, over a flat board.

Wet method – acrylics and wool/acrylic mixes

Using rustproof pins, pin the crochet fabric to the correct measurements on a flat surface and dampen using a spray bottle of cold water. Pat the fabric to help the moisture penetrate. Ease stitches into position, keeping rows and stitches straight. Allow to dry before removing the pins.

Steam method – wools and cottons

Pin out the fabric as above. For fabric with raised stitches, pin it right side up to avoid squashing the stitches; otherwise, pin it wrong side up. Steam lightly, holding the iron 2.5cm (1in) above the fabric. Allow the steam to penetrate for several seconds. It is safer to avoid pressing, but if you choose to do so, cover with a clean towel or cloth first.

Joining and Edging

If you are making your project from a block pattern, you will need to sew or crochet the blocks together. Although most of the projects in this book don't require an edging, you'll find simple instructions here if you choose to add an edging to your finished throw. A crochet edging does not just finish off a project with style, but it also helps your project to hold its shape and keeps the edges from stretching.

JOINING BLOCKS

Blocks can be joined by sewing or by crochet. Pin seams together to help match up the blocks and give a neat finish. Use the same yarn that you used for the blocks, or a finer yarn, preferably with the same fibre content.

Backstitch
Hold the blocks with right sides together. Using a yarn needle, work a line of backstitches along the edge.

Crochet seams
Join the blocks with wrong sides together for a visible seam, or with right sides together for an invisible one. Work a row of slip stitch (above) or double crochet through both top loops of each block.

SIMPLE EDGING

Working a simple round of double crochet stitches helps to even out untidy edges at row ends and any uneven stitches. Make a simple edging by crocheting one round of double crochet around the throw, working three stitches in each corner.

Oversewing
Using a yarn needle, sew through the back or front loops of corresponding stitches. For extra strength, work two stitches into the end loops.

Mattress stitch
Lay the blocks right side up and with edges touching. Using a yarn needle, weave back and forth around the centres of the stitches, without pulling them too tight.

Reading Charts

Charts are read from the bottom-right corner and worked left diagonally. Each square of the chart represents one block of the pattern and shows which colour to use.

Along sides of stitches

When working along the side of stitches, insert the hook under two threads of the first (or last) stitch of each row. Place the stitches an even distance apart along the edge. Try a short length to test the number of stitches required for a flat result. As a guide:

- Double crochet: 1 dc in side edge of each stitch.
- Treble crochet: 2 dc in side edge of each stitch.

Across the top or bottom of stitches

When working across the top of stitches, work 1 dc into each stitch as you would if working another row. When working across chain stitches, work 1 dc in the remaining loop of each chain.

Around corners

You will need to add a couple of stitches at each corner to allow the edging to turn the corner without distorting the block. As a guide, corners are normally turned by working 3 dc into the corner. If you want to add a larger or more complex edging and find that the base round is too wavy or too taut after it has been completed, it will probably get worse once the rest of the edging has been worked. Take time at this point to pull out the base round and redo it using fewer stitches if the edge is too wavy, or using more stitches if the edge is too taut.

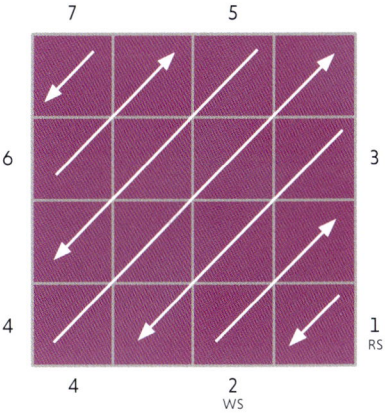

Row 1 (RS) is worked from right to left: crochet 1 block.

Row 2 (WS) is worked from left to right: crochet 2 blocks.

Row 3 (RS) is worked from right to left: crochet 3 blocks.

Continue reading the chart back and forth in diagonal rows, crocheting blocks of colour as indicated on the chart. Work increases until you reach the widest part of the chart, then continue crocheting back and forth, working decrease rows and ending in the top-left corner.

Tip: It's useful to attach a stitch marker or scrap of yarn to the right side of your project so it's easier to keep track of where you are.

chapter 2

BLANKET
PATTERNS

Reflection

This is a modern design worked in soft colours. This pattern would look great in bolder colours too. Try adding tassels at either end for a lovely finish.

SKILL LEVEL

☐ ☐ ☐

HOOK SIZE

6mm (US J-10)

BLOCK STITCH

3 tr block: (3 ch, 3 tr in ch sp)

THROW SIZE

110 x 160cm (43¼ x 63in)

YARN

Cascade 220® (aran/10-ply/worsted; 100g/3½oz; 200m/219yd)

A	8010 Natural – 8 balls	
B	9668 Paprika – 2 balls	
C	1048 Camelia – 2 balls	
D	1070 Golden Kiwi – 1 ball	
E	1054 Mallard Blue – 1 ball	
F	8400 Charcoal Grey – 1 ball	

ABBREVIATIONS & STITCHES

ch	chain
ch sp	chain space
dec	sl st in next 3 sts, sl st into 3-ch sp
inc	ch 6, 1 tr in fourth ch from hook, 1 tr in next 2 ch, sl st into ch sp of next block
rep	repeat
RS	right side
sl st	slip stitch
st(s)	stitch(es)
tr	treble crochet
WS	wrong side
↙/↗	direction of work

Throw

- ↙ Row 1 (RS): using yarn A, ch 6, 1 tr in third ch from hook and in next 2 ch, turn (1 block).
- ↗ Row 2 (WS): inc, A x 1, turn (2 blocks).
- ↙ Row 3 (RS): inc, A x 2, turn (3 blocks).
- ↗ Row 4 (WS): inc, A x 3, turn (4 blocks).
- ↙ Row 5 (RS): inc, A x 4, turn (5 blocks).
- ↗ Row 6 (WS): inc, A x 5, turn (6 blocks).
- ↙ Row 7 (RS): inc, A x 6, turn (7 blocks).
- ↗ Row 8 (WS): inc, A x 7, turn (8 blocks).
- ↙ Row 9 (RS): inc, A x 8, turn (9 blocks).
- ↗ Row 10 (WS): inc, A x 8, B x 1, turn (10 blocks).
- ↙ Row 11 (RS): inc in B, A x 10, turn (11 blocks).
- ↗ Row 12 (WS): inc, A x 9, B x 2, turn (12 blocks).
- ↙ Row 13 (RS): inc, B x 1, A x 11, turn (13 blocks).
- ↗ Row 14 (WS): inc, A x 10, B x 3, turn (14 blocks).
- ↙ Row 15 (RS): inc, B x 2, A x 12, turn (15 blocks).
- ↗ Row 16 (WS): inc, A x 11, B x 3, C x 1, turn (16 blocks).
- ↙ Row 17 (RS): inc in C, B x 3, A x 13, turn (17 blocks).
- ↗ Row 18 (WS): inc, A x 12, B x 3, C x 2, turn (18 blocks).
- ↙ Row 19 (RS): inc, C x 1, B x 3, A x 14, turn (19 blocks).
- ↗ Row 20 (WS): inc, A x 13, B x 3, C x 3, turn (20 blocks).
- ↙ Row 21 (RS): inc, C x 2, B x 3, A x 15, turn (21 blocks).
- ↗ Row 22 (WS): inc, A x 14, B x 3, C x 3, D x 1, turn (22 blocks).
- ↙ Row 23 (RS): inc in D, C x 3, B x 3, A x 16, turn (23 blocks).
- ↗ Row 24 (WS): inc, A x 15, B x 3, C x 3, D x 2, turn (24 blocks).
- ↙ Row 25 (RS): inc, D x 1, C x 3, B x 3, A x 17, turn (25 blocks).
- ↗ Row 26 (WS): inc, A x 16, B x 3, C x 3, D x 3, turn (26 blocks).
- ↙ Row 27 (RS): inc, D x 2, C x 3, B x 3, A x 18, turn (27 blocks).
- ↗ Row 28 (WS): inc, A x 17, B x 3, C x 3, D x 3, E x 1, turn (28 blocks).

- ↙ Row 29 (RS): inc in E, D x 3, C x 3, B x 3, A x 19, turn (29 blocks).
- ↗ Row 30 (WS): inc, A x 18, B x 3, C x 3, D x 3, E x 2, turn (30 blocks).
- ↙ Row 31 (RS): inc, E x 2, D x 3, C x 3, B x 3, A x 20, turn (31 blocks).
- ↗ Row 32 (WS): inc, A x 29, B x 3, C x 3, D x 3, E x 3, turn (32 blocks).
- ↙ Row 33 (RS): inc, E x 2, D x 3, C x 3, B x 3, A x 21, turn (33 blocks).
- ↗ Row 34 (WS): inc, A x 20, B x 3, C x 3, D x 3, E x 3, F x 1, turn (34 blocks).
- ↙ Row 35 (RS): inc in F, E x 3, D x 3, C x 3, B x 3, A x 22, turn (35 blocks).
- ↗ Row 36 (WS): inc, A x 21, B x 3, C x 3, D x 3, E x 3, F x 2, turn (36 blocks).
- ↙ Row 37 (RS): inc, F x 1, E x 3, D x 3, C x 3, B x 3, A x 23, turn (37 blocks).
- ↗ Row 38 (WS): inc, A x 22, B x 3, C x 3, D x 3, E x 3, F x 3, turn (38 blocks).
- ↙ Row 39 (RS): inc, F x 2, E x 3, D x 3, C x 3, B x 3, A x 24, turn (39 blocks).
- ↗ Row 40 (WS): inc, A x 23, B x 3, C x 3, D x 3, E x 3, F x 4, fasten off yarn F, turn (40 blocks).
- ↙ Row 41 (RS): inc, E x 6, D x 3, C x 3, B x 3, A x 25, turn (41 blocks).
- ↗ Row 42 (WS): inc, A x 24, B x 3, C x 3, D x 3, E x 8, turn (42 blocks).
- ↙ Row 43 (RS): inc, E x 7, D x 3, C x 3, B x 3, A x 26, turn (43 blocks).
- ↗ Row 44 (WS): inc, A x 25, B x 3, C x 3, D x 3, E x 9, turn (44 blocks).
- ↙ Row 45 (RS): inc, E x 8, D x 3, C x 3, B x 3, A x 27, turn (45 blocks).
- ↗ Row 46 (WS): inc, A x 26, B x 3, C x 3, D x 3, E x 10, fasten off yarn E, turn (46 blocks).
- ↙ Row 47 (RS): inc, D x 12, C x 3, B x 3, A x 28, turn (47 blocks).
- ↗ Row 48 (WS): inc, A x 27, B x 3, C x 3, D x 14, turn (48 blocks).
- ↙ Row 49 (RS): inc, D x 13, C x 3, B x 3, A x 29, turn (49 blocks).
- ↗ Row 50 (WS): inc, A x 28, B x 3, C x 3, D x 15, turn (50 blocks).
- ↙ Row 51 (RS): inc, D x 14, C x 3, B x 3, A x 30, turn (51 blocks).
- ↗ Row 52 (WS): inc, A x 29, B x 3, C x 3, D x 16, fasten off yarn D, turn (52 blocks).
- ↙ Row 53 (RS): inc, C x 18, B x 3, A x 31, turn (53 blocks).

- ↗ Row 54 (WS): inc, A x 30, B x 3, C x 20, turn (54 blocks).
- ↙ Row 55 (RS): inc, C x 19, B x 3, A x 32, turn (55 blocks).

Corner: start decreasing on WS.

- ↗ Row 56 (WS): dec, A x 31, B x 3, C x 21, turn (55 blocks).
- ↙ Row 57 (RS): inc, C x 20, B x 3, A x 31, turn (55 blocks).
- ↗ Row 58 (WS): dec, A x 30, B x 3, C x 22, fasten off yarn C, turn (55 blocks).
- ↙ Row 59 (RS): inc, B x 24, A x 30, turn (55 blocks).
- ↗ Row 60 (WS): dec, A x 29, B x 26, turn (55 blocks).
- ↙ Row 61 (RS): inc, B x 25, A x 29, turn (55 blocks).
- ↗ Row 62 (WS): dec, A x 28, B x 27, turn (55 blocks).
- ↙ Row 63 (RS): inc, B x 26, A x 28, turn (55 blocks).
- ↗ Row 64 (WS): dec, B x 55, turn (55 blocks).
- ↙ Row 65 (RS): inc, A x 27, B x 27, turn (55 blocks).
- ↗ Row 66 (WS): dec, B x 27, A x 28, turn (55 blocks).
- ↙ Row 67 (RS): inc, A x 28, B x 26, turn (55 blocks).
- ↗ Row 68 (WS): dec, B x 26, A x 29, turn (55 blocks).
- ↙ Row 69 (RS): inc, A x 29, B x 25, fasten off yarn B, turn (55 blocks).
- ↗ Row 70 (WS): dec, C x 22, B x 3, A x 30, turn (55 blocks).
- ↙ Row 71 (RS): inc, A x 30, B x 3, C x 21, turn (55 blocks).
- ↗ Row 72 (WS): dec, C x 21, B x 3, A x 31, turn (55 blocks).
- ↙ Row 73 (RS): inc, A x 31, B x 3, C x 20, turn (55 blocks).
- ↗ Row 74 (WS): dec, C x 20, B x 3, A x 32, turn (55 blocks).
- ↙ Row 75 (RS): inc, A x 32, B x 3, C x 19, fasten off yarn C, turn (55 blocks).

Corner: start decreasing on RS.

- ↗ Row 76 (WS): dec, D x 16, C x 3, B x 3, A x 32, turn (54 blocks).
- ↙ Row 77 (RS): dec, A x 32, B x 3, C x 3, D x 15, turn (53 blocks).

↗ Row 78 (WS): dec, D x 15, C x 3, B x 3, A x 31, turn (52 blocks).

↙ Row 79 (RS): dec, A x 31, B x 3, C x 3, D x 14, turn (51 blocks).

↗ Row 80 (WS): dec, D x 14, C x 3, B x 3, A x 30, turn (50 blocks).

↙ Row 81 (RS): dec, A x 30, B x 3, C x 3, D x 13, fasten off yarn D, turn (49 blocks).

↗ Row 82 (WS): dec, E x 10, D x 3, C x 3, B x 3, A x 29, turn (48 blocks).

↙ Row 83 (RS): dec, A x 29, B x 3, C x 3, D x 3, E x 9, turn (47 blocks).

↗ Row 84 (WS): dec, E x 9, D x 3, C x 3, B x 3, A x 28, turn (46 blocks).

↙ Row 85 (RS): dec, A x 28, B x 3, C x 3, D x 3, E x 8, turn (45 blocks).

↗ Row 86 (WS): dec, E x 8, D x 3, C x 3, B x 3, A x 27, turn (44 blocks).

↙ Row 87 (RS): dec, A x 27, B x 3, C x 3, D x 3, E x 7, fasten off yarn E, turn (43 blocks).

↗ Row 88 (WS): dec, F x 4, E x 3, D x 3, C x 3, B x 3, A x 26, turn (42 blocks).

↙ Row 89 (RS): dec, A x 26, B x 3, C x 3, D x 3, E x 3, F x 3, turn (41 blocks).

↗ Row 90 (WS): dec, F x 3, E x 3, D x 3, C x 3, B x 3, A x 25, turn (40 blocks).

↙ Row 91 (RS): dec, A x 25, B x 3, C x 3, D x 3, E x 3, F x 2, turn (39 blocks).

↗ Row 92 (WS): dec, F x 2, E x 3, D x 3, C x 3, B x 3, A x 24, turn (38 blocks).

↙ Row 93 (RS): dec, A x 24, B x 3, C x 3, D x 3, E x 3, F x 1, turn (37 blocks).

↗ Row 94 (WS): dec, F x 1, E x 3, D x 3, C x 3, B x 3, A x 23, fasten off yarn F, turn (36 blocks).

↙ Row 95 (RS): dec, A x 23, B x 3, C x 3, D x 3, E x 3, turn (35 blocks).

↗ Row 96 (WS): dec, E x 3, D x 3, C x 3, B x 3, A x 22, turn (34 blocks).

↙ Row 97 (RS): dec, A x 22, B x 3, C x 3, D x 3, E x 2, turn (33 blocks).

↗ Row 98 (WS): dec, E x 2, D x 3, C x 3, B x 3, A x 21, turn (32 blocks).

↙ Row 99 (RS): dec, A x 21, B x 3, C x 3, D x 3, E x 1, turn (31 blocks).

↗ Row 100 (WS): dec, E x 1, D x 3, C x 3, B x 3, A x 20, fasten off yarn E, turn (30 blocks).

↙ Row 101 (RS): dec, A x 20, B x 3, C x 3, D x 3, turn (29 blocks).

↗ Row 102 (WS): dec, D x 3, C x 3, B x 3, A x 19, turn (28 blocks).

↙ Row 103 (RS): dec, A x 19, B x 3, C x 3, D x 2, turn (27 blocks).

↗ Row 104 (WS): dec, D x 2, C x 3, B x 3, A x 18, turn (26 blocks).

↙ Row 105 (RS): dec, A x 18, B x 3, C x 3, D x 1, turn (25 blocks).

↗ Row 106 (WS): dec, D x 1, C x 3, B x 3, A x 17, fasten off yarn D, turn (24 blocks).

↙ Row 107 (RS): dec, A x 17, B x 3, C x 3, turn (23 blocks).

↗ Row 108 (WS): dec, C x 3, B x 3, A x 16, turn (22 blocks).

↙ Row 109 (RS): dec, A x 16, B x 3, C x 2, turn (21 blocks).

↗ Row 110 (WS): dec, C x 2, B x 3, A x 15, turn (20 blocks).

↙ Row 111 (RS): dec, A x 15, B x 3, C x 1, turn (19 blocks).

↗ Row 112 (WS): dec, C x 1, B x 3, A x 14, fasten off yarn C, turn (18 blocks).

↙ Row 113 (RS): dec, A x 14, B x 3, turn (17 blocks).

↗ Row 114 (WS): dec, B x 3, A x 13, turn (16 blocks).

↙ Row 115 (RS): dec, A x 13, B x 2, turn (15 blocks).

↗ Row 116 (WS): dec, B x 2, A x 12, turn (14 blocks).

↙ Row 117 (RS): dec, A x 12, B x 1, turn (13 blocks).

↗ Row 118 (WS): dec, B x 1, A x 11, fasten off yarn B, turn (12 blocks).

↙ Row 119 (RS): dec, A x 11, turn (11 blocks).

↗ Row 120 (WS): dec, A x 10, turn (10 blocks).

↙ Row 121 (RS): dec, A x 9, turn (9 blocks).

↗ Row 122 (WS): dec, A x 8, turn (8 blocks).

↙ Row 123 (RS): dec, A x 7, turn (7 blocks).

↗ Row 124 (WS): dec, A x 6, turn (6 blocks).

↙ Row 125 (RS): dec, A x 5, turn (5 blocks).

↗ Row 126 (WS): dec, A x 4, turn (4 blocks).

↙ Row 127 (RS): dec, A x 3, turn (3 blocks).

↗ Row 128 (WS): dec, A x 2, turn (2 blocks).

↙ Row 129 (RS): dec, A x 1, fasten off yarn A (1 block).

Sew in all loose ends on WS of work.

California Retro

The warm colours used in this throw conjure up a sandy beach with colourful bathing costumes and sun umbrellas. It is easy to make and a great project for beginners to the corner-to-corner technique.

YARN

Cascade 220 Superwash® (DK/8-ply/light worsted; 100g/3½oz; 200m/220yd)

	A	349 Irish Cream – 2 balls
	B	817 Ecru – 2 balls
	C	259 Blue Turquoise – 2 balls
	D	226 Peppermint – 2 balls
	E	287 Deep Sea Coral – 2 balls
	F	820 Lemon – 1 ball

ABBREVIATIONS & STITCHES

ch	chain
ch sp	chain space
dec	sl st in next 3 sts, sl st into 3-ch sp
inc	ch 6, 1 tr in fourth ch from hook, 1 tr in next 2 ch, sl st into ch sp of next block
rep	repeat
RS	right side
sl st	slip stitch
st(s)	stitch(es)
tr	treble crochet
WS	wrong side
↙ / ↗	direction of work

Throw

↙ Row 1 (RS): using yarn A, ch 6, 1 tr in fourth ch from hook and in next 2 ch, turn (1 block).

↗ Row 2 (WS): inc, A x 1, turn (2 blocks).

↙ Row 3 (RS): inc, A x 2, turn (3 blocks).

↗ Row 4 (WS): inc, A x 3, turn (4 blocks).

↙ Row 5 (RS): inc, A x 4, turn (5 blocks).

↗ Row 6 (WS): inc, A x 5, turn (6 blocks).

↙ Row 7 (RS): inc, A x 6, turn (7 blocks).

↗ Row 8 (WS): inc, A x 7, fasten off yarn A, turn (8 blocks).

↙ Row 9 (RS): join yarn B, inc, B x 8, turn (9 blocks).

↗ Row 10 (WS): inc, B x 9, turn (10 blocks).

↙ Row 11 (RS): inc, B x 10, turn (11 blocks).

↗ Row 12 (WS): inc, B x 11, fasten off yarn B, turn (12 blocks).

↙ Row 13 (RS): join yarn C, inc, C x 12, turn (13 blocks).

↗ Row 14 (WS): inc, C x 13, turn (14 blocks).

↙ Row 15 (RS): inc, C x 14, turn (15 blocks).

↗ Row 16 (WS): inc, C x 15, turn (16 blocks).

↙ Row 17 (RS): inc, C x 16, turn (17 blocks).

↗ Row 18 (WS): inc, C x 17, fasten off yarn C, turn (18 blocks).

↙ Row 19 (RS): join yarn B, inc, B x 18, turn (19 blocks).

↗ Row 20 (WS): inc, B x 19, turn (20 blocks).

↙ Row 21 (RS): inc, B x 20, turn (21 blocks).

↗ Row 22 (WS): inc, B x 21, fasten off yarn B, turn (22 blocks).

↙ Row 23 (RS): join yarn D, inc, D x 22, turn (23 blocks).

↗ Row 24 (WS): inc, D x 23, turn (24 blocks).

↙ Row 25 (RS): inc, D x 24, turn (25 blocks).

↗ Row 26 (WS): inc, D x 25, turn (26 blocks).

↙ Row 27 (RS): inc, D x 26, turn (27 blocks).

↗ Row 28 (WS): inc, D x 27, fasten off yarn D, turn (28 blocks).

↙ Row 29 (RS): join yarn B, inc, B x 28, turn (29 blocks).

↗ Row 30 (WS): inc, B x 29, turn (30 blocks).

↙ Row 31 (RS): inc, B x 30, turn (31 blocks).

↗ Row 32 (WS): inc, B x 31, fasten off yarn B, turn (32 blocks).

↙ Row 33 (RS): join yarn E, inc, E x 32, turn (33 blocks).

↗ Row 34 (WS): inc, E x 33, turn (34 blocks).

↙ Row 35 (RS): inc, E x 34, turn (35 blocks).

↗ Row 36 (WS): inc, E x 35, turn (36 blocks).

↙ Row 37 (RS): inc, E x 36, turn (37 blocks).

↗ Row 38 (WS): inc, E x 37, fasten off yarn E, turn (38 blocks).

↙ Row 39 (RS): join yarn B, inc, B x 38, turn (39 blocks).

↗ Row 40 (WS): inc, B x 39, turn (40 blocks).

↙ Row 41 (RS): inc, B x 40, turn (41 blocks).

↗ Row 42 (WS): inc, B x 41, fasten off yarn B, turn (42 blocks).

↙ Row 43 (RS): join yarn F, inc, F x 42, turn (43 blocks).

↗ Row 44 (WS): inc, F x 43, turn (44 blocks).

↙ Row 45 (RS): inc, F x 44, turn (45 blocks).

↗ Row 46 (WS): inc, F x 45, turn (46 blocks).

↙ Row 47 (RS): inc, F x 46, turn (47 blocks).

↗ Row 48 (WS): inc, F x 47, fasten off yarn F, turn (48 blocks).

↙ Row 49 (RS): join yarn B, inc, B x 48, turn (49 blocks).

↗ Row 50 (WS): inc, B x 49, turn (50 blocks).

↙ Row 51 (RS): inc, B x 50, turn (51 blocks).

↗ Row 52 (WS): inc, B x 51, fasten off yarn B, turn (52 blocks).

↙ Row 53 (RS): join yarn G, inc, G x 52, turn (53 blocks).

↗ Row 54 (WS): inc, G x 53, turn (54 blocks).

↙ Row 55 (RS): inc, G x 54, turn (55 blocks).

↗ Row 56 (WS): inc, G x 55, turn (56 blocks).

↙ Row 57 (RS): inc, G x 56, turn (57 blocks).

↗ Row 58 (WS): inc, G x 57, turn (58 blocks).

↙ Row 59 (RS): inc, G x 58, turn (59 blocks).

Corner: start decreasing on WS.

↗ Row 60 (WS): dec, G x 58, turn (59 blocks).

↙ Row 61 (RS): inc, G x 58, turn (59 blocks).

Rows 63–88: rep rows 60 and 61.

↗ Row 88 (WS): dec, G x 58, turn (59 blocks).

Corner: start decreasing on RS.

↙ Row 89 (RS): dec, G x 57, turn (58 blocks).

↗ Row 90 (WS): dec, G x 56, turn (57 blocks).

↙ Row 91 (RS): dec, G x 55, turn (56 blocks).

↗ Row 92 (WS): dec, G x 54, turn (55 blocks).

↙ Row 93 (RS): dec, G x 53, turn (54 blocks).

↗ Row 94 (WS): dec, G x 52, turn (53 blocks).

↙ Row 95 (RS): dec, G x 51, turn (52 blocks).

↗ Row 96 (WS): dec, G x 50, turn (51 blocks).

↙ Row 97 (RS): dec, G x 49, turn (50 blocks).

↗ Row 98 (WS): dec, G x 48, turn (49 blocks).

↙ Row 99 (RS): dec, G x 47, turn (48 blocks).

↗ Row 100 (WS): dec, G x 46, turn (47 blocks).

↙ Row 101 (RS): dec, G x 45, turn (46 blocks).

↗ Row 102 (WS): dec, G x 44, turn (45 blocks).

↙ Row 103 (RS): dec, G x 43, turn (44 blocks).

↗ Row 104 (WS): dec, G x 42, turn (43 blocks).

↙ Row 105 (RS): dec, G x 41, turn (42 blocks).

↗ Row 106 (WS): dec, G x 40, turn (41 blocks).

↙ Row 107 (RS): dec, G x 39, turn (40 blocks).

↗ Row 108 (WS): dec, G x 38, turn (39 blocks).

↙ Row 109 (RS): dec, G x 37, turn (38 blocks).

↗ Row 110 (WS): dec, G x 36, turn (37 blocks).

↙ Row 111 (RS): dec, G x 35, turn (36 blocks).

↗ Row 112 (WS): dec, G x 34, turn (35 blocks).

↙ Row 113 (RS): dec, G x 33, turn (34 blocks).

↗ Row 114 (WS): dec, G x 32, turn (33 blocks).

↙ Row 115 (RS): dec, G x 31, fasten off yarn G, turn (32 blocks).

↗ Row 116 (WS): join yarn B in ch sp of last block made, B x 30, turn (31 blocks).

↙ Row 117 (RS): dec, B x 29, fasten off yarn B, turn (30 blocks).

↗ Row 118 (WS): join yarn F in ch sp of last block made, F x 28, turn (29 blocks).

↙ Row 119 (RS): dec, F x 27, turn (28 blocks).

↗ Row 120 (WS): dec, F x 26, fasten off yarn F, turn (27 blocks).

↙ Row 121 (RS): join yarn B in ch sp of last block made, B x 25, turn (26 blocks).

↗ Row 122 (WS): dec, B x 24, fasten off yarn B, turn (25 blocks).

↙ Row 123 (RS): join yarn E in ch sp of last block made, E x 23, turn (24 blocks).

↗ Row 124 (WS): dec, E x 22, turn (23 blocks).

↙ Row 125 (RS): dec, E x 21, fasten off yarn B, turn (22 blocks).

↗ Row 126 (WS): join yarn B in ch sp of last block made, B x 20, turn (21 blocks).

↙ Row 127 (RS): dec, B x 19, fasten off yarn B, turn (20 blocks).

↗ Row 128 (WS): join yarn D in ch sp of last block made, D x 18, turn (19 blocks).

↙ Row 129 (RS): dec, D x 17, turn (18 blocks).

↗ Row 130 (WS): dec, D x 16, fasten off yarn D, turn (17 blocks).

↙ Row 131 (RS): join yarn B in ch sp of last block made, B x 15, turn (16 blocks).

↗ Row 132 (WS): dec, B x 14, fasten off yarn B, turn (15 blocks).

↙ Row 133 (RS): join yarn C in ch sp of last block made, C x 13, turn (14 blocks).

↗ Row 134 (WS): dec, C x 12, turn, turn (13 blocks).

↙ Row 135 (RS): dec, C x 11, fasten off yarn C (12 blocks).

↗ Row 136 (WS): join yarn B in ch sp of last block made, B x 10, turn (11 blocks).

↙ Row 137 (RS): dec, B x 9, fasten off yarn B, turn (10 blocks).

↗ Row 138 (WS): join yarn A in ch sp of last block made, A x 8, turn (9 blocks).

↙ Row 139 (RS): dec, A x 7, turn (8 blocks).

↗ Row 140 (WS): dec, A x 6, turn (7 blocks).

↙ Row 141 (RS): dec, A x 5, turn (6 blocks).

↗ Row 142 (WS): dec, A x 4, turn (5 blocks).

↙ Row 143 (RS): dec, A x 3, turn (4 blocks).

↗ Row 144 (WS): dec, A x 2, turn (3 blocks).

↙ Row 145 (RS): dec, A x 1, turn (2 blocks).

↗ Row 146 (WS): dec, A x 1, fasten off yarn A (1 block).

Sew in all loose ends on WS of work.

Copenhagen

Crochet individual squares and join them together at the end to create this simple throw. If you'd like to make a larger throw, use the yarn requirements per square to calculate how much extra yarn you'll need.

SKILL LEVEL

■ □ □

HOOK SIZE

5mm (US H-8)

BLOCK STITCH

3 tr block: (3 ch, 3 tr in ch sp)

SQUARE SIZE

19 x 19cm (7½ x 7½in)

THROW SIZE

76 x 114cm (30 x 45in)

YARN

Cascade 220 Superwash® (DK/8-ply/light worsted; 100g/3½oz; 200m/220yd)

A	877 Golden – 1 ball
B	817 Ecru – 5 balls
C	1941 Salmon – 1 ball
D	314 Garnet – 1 ball
E	811 Como Blue – 1 ball

Yarn per square

A	5m (5½yd)
B	35m (38yd)
C	7.5m (8yd)
D	7.5m (8yd)
E	5m (5½yd)

ABBREVIATIONS & STITCHES

ch	chain
ch sp	chain space
dc	double crochet
dec	sl st in next 3 sts, sl st into 3-ch sp
inc	ch 6, 1 tr in fourth ch from hook, 1 tr in next 2 ch, sl st into next ch sp
rep	repeat
RS	right side
sl st	slip stitch
st(s)	stitch(es)
tr	treble crochet
WS	wrong side
↙/↗	direction of work
[ ]	repeat instructions between brackets number of times stated

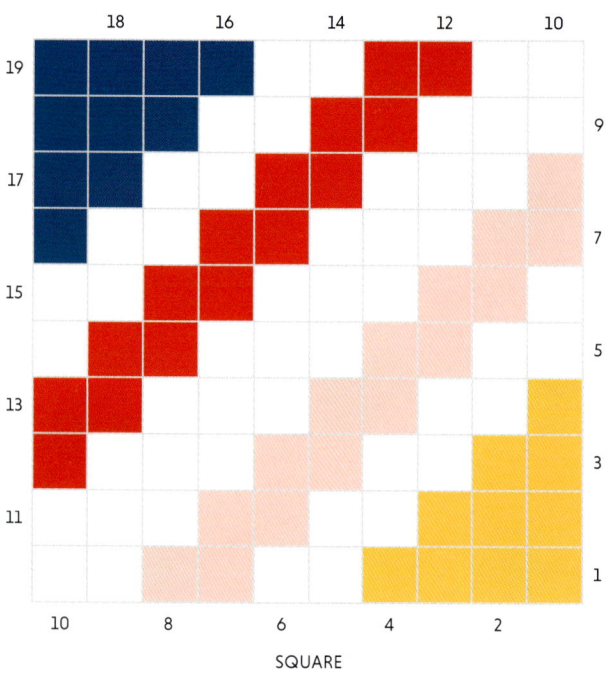

Square

Make 24 squares

↙ **Row 1 (RS):** using yarn A, ch 6, 1 tr in fourth ch from hook and in next 2 ch, turn (1 block).

↗ **Row 2 (WS):** inc, A x 1, turn (2 blocks).

↙ **Row 3 (RS):** inc, A x 2, turn (3 blocks).

↗ **Row 4 (WS):** inc, A x 3, fasten off yarn A, turn (4 blocks).

↙ **Row 5 (RS):** join yarn B, inc, B x 4, turn (5 blocks).

↗ **Row 6 (WS):** inc, B x 5, fasten off yarn B, turn (6 blocks).

↙ **Row 7 (RS):** join yarn C, inc, C x 6, turn (7 blocks).

↗ **Row 8 (WS):** inc, C x 7, fasten off yarn C, turn (8 blocks).

↙ **Row 9 (RS):** inc, B x 8, turn (9 blocks).

↗ **Row 10 (WS):** inc, B x 9, turn (10 blocks).

Now decrease at start of each row.

↙ **Row 11 (WS):** dec, B x 9, fasten off yarn B, turn (9 blocks).

↙ **Row 12 (RS):** dec, D x 8, turn (8 blocks).

↗ **Row 13 (WS):** dec, D x 7, fasten off yarn D, turn (7 blocks).

↙ **Row 14 (RS):** dec, B x 6, turn (6 blocks).

↗ **Row 15 (WS):** dec, B x 5, fasten off yarn B, turn (5 blocks).

↙ **Row 16 (RS):** dec, E x 4, turn (4 blocks).

↗ **Row 17 (WS):** dec, E x 3, turn (3 blocks)

↙ **Row 18 (RS):** dec, E x 2, turn (2 blocks).

↗ **Row 19 (WS):** dec, E x 1, fasten off yarn E, turn (1 block).

Edging

Row 1 (RS): join yarn B in any corner st, ch 1, 1 dc in same place, [ch 2, 1 dc in next gap between two blocks] nine times, ch 2, 1 dc in corner st] four times omitting last dc, join with sl st to first dc made.

Row 2 (RS): ch 1, [3 dc in corner st, [2 dc in ch-2 sp, 1 dc in dc] nine times, 2 dc in ch-2 sp] four times, join with sl st to first st made, fasten off yarn B.

Sew in all loose ends on WS of work.

Throw

Joining

Following the layout chart, crochet the squares together in 6 rows of 4 squares. Use yarn B and the sl st through the back loop method.

Sew in all loose ends on WS of work.

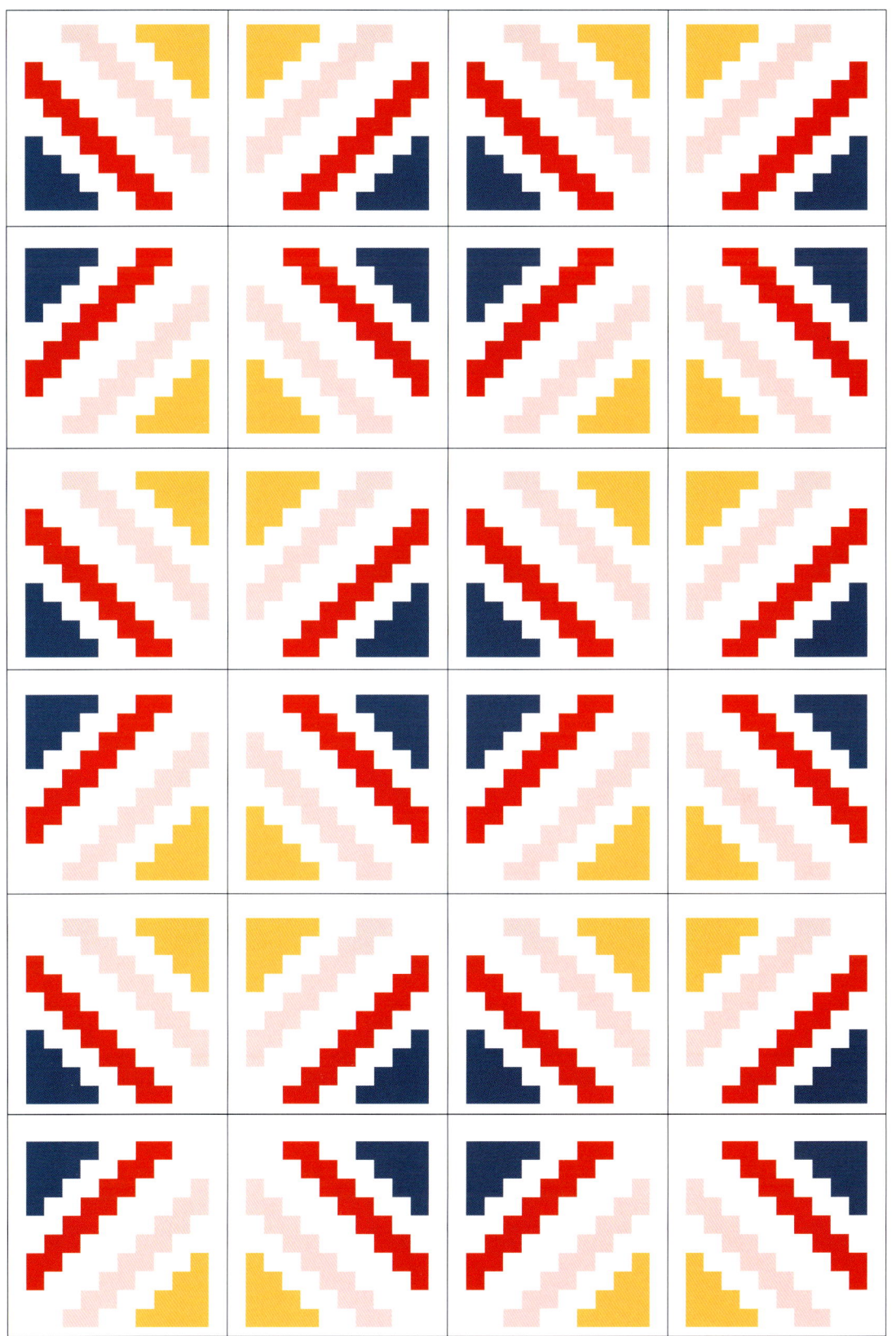

SQUARE LAYOUT CHART

Rainbow in a Grey Sky

This is a super-easy blanket to make with no colour changes mid-row. Work it in rainbow colours, or try working an ombre for a beautiful effect.

SKILL LEVEL

■ □ □

HOOK SIZE

6mm (US J-10)

BLOCK STITCH

3 tr block: (3 ch, 3 tr in ch sp)

THROW SIZE

110 x 160cm (43¼ x 63in)

YARN

Cascade 220® (aran/10-ply/worsted; 100g/3½oz; 200m/219yd)

	A	1058 Nimbus Cloud – 3 balls
	B	8505 White – 2 balls
	C	9668 Paprika – 1 ball
	D	1048 Camelia – 1 ball
	E	9463B Gold – 2 balls
	F	8910 Citron – 2 balls
	G	1072 Key West – 2 balls
	H	8951 Aqua – 2 balls
	I	8762 Deep Lavender – 2 balls

ABBREVIATIONS & STITCHES

ch	chain
ch sp	chain space
dec	sl st in next 3 sts, sl st into 3-ch sp
inc	ch 6, 1 tr in fourth ch from hook, 1 tr in next 2 ch, sl st into ch sp of next block
rep	repeat
RS	right side
sl st	slip stitch
st(s)	stitch(es)
tr	treble crochet
WS	wrong side
↙ / ↗	direction of work

Throw

Row 1 (RS): using yarn A, ch 6, 1 tr in third ch from hook and next 2 ch, turn (1 block).

↗ Row 2 (WS): inc, A x 1, turn (2 blocks).

↙ Row 3 (RS): inc, A x 2, turn (3 blocks).

↗ Row 4 (WS): inc, A x 3, turn (4 blocks).

↙ Row 5 (RS): inc, A x 4, turn (5 blocks).

↗ Row 6 (WS): inc, A x 5, turn (6 blocks).

↙ Row 7 (RS): inc, A x 6, turn (7 blocks).

↗ Row 8 (WS): inc, A x 7, turn (8 blocks).

↙ Row 9 (RS): inc, A x 8, turn (9 blocks).

↗ Row 10 (WS): inc, A x 9, turn (10 blocks).

↙ Row 11 (RS): inc, A x 10, turn (11 blocks).

↗ Row 12 (WS): inc, A x 11, turn (12 blocks).

↙ Row 13 (RS): inc, A x 12, turn (13 blocks).

↗ Row 14 (WS): inc, A x 13, turn (14 blocks).

↙ Row 15 (RS): inc, A x 14, turn (15 blocks).

↗ Row 16 (WS): inc, A x 15, turn (16 blocks).

↙ Row 17 (RS): inc, A x 16, turn (17 blocks).

↗ Row 18 (WS): inc, A x 17, turn (18 blocks).

↙ Row 19 (RS): inc, A x 18 changing to yarn B when working last st, fasten off yarn A, turn (19 blocks).

↗ Row 20 (WS): inc, B x 19, turn (20 blocks).

↙ Row 21 (RS): inc, B x 20, turn (21 blocks).

↗ Row 22 (WS): inc, B x 21, turn (22 blocks).

↙ Row 23 (RS): inc, B x 22, turn (23 blocks).

↗ Row 24 (WS): inc, B x 23, turn (24 blocks).

↙ Row 25 (RS): inc, B x 24, turn (25 blocks).

↗ Row 26 (WS): inc, B x 25, turn (26 blocks).

↙ Row 27 (RS): inc, B x 26, turn (27 blocks).

↗ Row 28 (WS): inc, B x 27, turn (28 blocks).

↙ Row 29 (RS): inc, B x 28 changing to yarn C when working last st, fasten off yarn B, turn (29 blocks).

↗ Row 30 (WS): inc, C x 29, turn (30 blocks).

↙ Row 31 (RS): inc, C x 30, turn (31 blocks).

↗ Row 32 (WS): inc, C x 31, turn (32 blocks).

↙ Row 33 (RS): inc, C x 32, turn (33 blocks).

↗ Row 34 (WS): inc, C x 33, turn (34 blocks).

↙ Row 35 (RS): inc, C x 34, turn (35 blocks).

↗ Row 36 (WS): inc, C x 35, turn (36 blocks).

↙ Row 37 (RS): inc, C x 36 changing to yarn D when working last st, fasten off yarn C, turn (37 blocks).

↗ Row 38 (WS): inc, D x 37, turn (38 blocks).

↙ Row 39 (RS): inc, D x 38, turn (39 blocks).

↗ Row 40 (WS): inc, D x 39, turn (40 blocks).

↙ Row 41 (RS): inc, D x 40, turn (41 blocks).

↗ Row 42 (WS): inc, D x 41, turn (42 blocks).

↙ Row 43 (RS): inc, D x 42, turn (43 blocks).

↗ Row 44 (WS): inc, D x 43, turn (44 blocks).

↙ Row 45 (RS): inc, D x 44 changing to yarn E when working last st, fasten off yarn D, turn (45 blocks).

↗ Row 46 (WS): inc, E x 45, turn (46 blocks).

↙ Row 47 (RS): inc, E x 46, turn (47 blocks).

↗ Row 48 (WS): inc, E x 47, turn (48 blocks).

↙ Row 49 (RS): inc, E x 48, turn (49 blocks).

↗ Row 50 (WS): inc, E x 49, turn (50 blocks).

↙ Row 51 (RS): inc, E x 50, turn (51 blocks).

↗ Row 52 (WS): inc, E x 51, turn (52 blocks).

↙ Row 53 (RS): inc, E x 52 changing to yarn F when working last st, fasten off yarn E, turn (53 blocks).

↗ Row 54 (WS): inc, F x 53, turn (54 blocks).

Corner: start decreasing on RS.

↙ Row 55 (RS): dec, F x 54, turn (54 blocks).

↗ Row 56 (WS): inc, F x 53, turn (54 blocks).

↙ Row 57 (RS): dec, F x 54, turn (54 blocks).

↗ Row 58 (WS): inc, F x 53, turn (54 blocks).

↙ Row 59 (RS): dec, F x 54, turn (54 blocks).

↗ Row 60 (WS): inc, F x 53, turn (54 blocks).

↙ Row 61 (RS): dec, F x 54 changing to yarn G when working last st, fasten off yarn F, turn (54 blocks).

↗ Row 62 (WS): inc, G x 53, turn (54 blocks).

↙ Row 63 (RS): dec, G x 54, turn (54 blocks).

↗ Row 64 (WS): inc, G x 53, turn (54 blocks).

↙ Row 65 (RS): dec, G x 54, turn (54 blocks).

↗ Row 66 (WS): inc, G x 53, turn (54 blocks).

↙ Row 67 (RS): dec, G x 54, turn (54 blocks).

↗ Row 68 (WS): inc, G x 53, turn (54 blocks).

↙ Row 69 (RS): dec, G x 54 changing to yarn H when working last st, fasten off yarn G, turn (54 blocks).

↗ Row 70 (WS): inc, H x 53, turn (54 blocks).

↙ Row 71 (RS): dec, H x 54, turn (54 blocks).

↗ Row 72 (WS): inc, H x 53, turn (54 blocks).

↙ Row 73 (RS): dec, H x 54, turn (54 blocks).

↗ Row 74 (WS): inc, H x 53, turn (54 blocks).

↙ Row 75 (RS): dec, H x 54, turn (54 blocks).

↗ Row 76 (WS): inc, H x 53, turn (54 blocks).

↙ Row 77 (RS): dec, H x 54 changing to yarn I when working last st, fasten off yarn H, turn (54 blocks).

↗ Row 78 (WS): inc, I x 53, turn (54 blocks).

Corner: start decreasing on WS.

↙ Row 79 (RS): dec, I x 53, turn (53 blocks).

↙ Row 80 (WS): dec, I x 52, turn (52 blocks).

↙ Row 81 (RS): dec, I x 51, turn (51 blocks).

↗ Row 82 (WS): dec, I x 50, turn (50 blocks).

↙ Row 83 (RS): dec, I x 49, turn (49 blocks).

↙ Row 84 (WS): dec, I x 48, turn (48 blocks).

↙ Row 85 (RS): dec, I x 47, fasten off yarn I, turn (47 blocks).

↗ Row 86 (WS): join yarn B in last ch sp made, B x 46, turn (46 blocks).

↙ Row 87 (RS): dec, B x 45, turn (45 blocks).

↗ Row 88 (WS): dec, B x 44, turn (44 blocks).

↙ Row 89 (RS): dec, B x 43, turn (43 blocks).

↙ Row 90 (WS): dec, B x 42, turn (42 blocks).

↙ Row 91 (RS): dec, B x 41, turn (41 blocks).

↗ Row 92 (WS): dec, B x 40, turn (40 blocks).

↙ Row 93 (RS): dec, B x 39, turn (39 blocks).

↗ Row 94 (WS): dec, B x 38, turn (38 blocks).

↙ Row 95 (RS): dec, B x 37, fasten off yarn B, turn (37 blocks).

↗ Row 96 (WS): join yarn A in last ch sp made, A x 36, turn (36 blocks).

↙ Row 97 (RS): dec, A x 35, turn (35 blocks).

↗ Row 98 (WS): dec, A x 34, turn (34 blocks).

↙ Row 99 (RS): dec, A x 33, turn (33 blocks).

↗ Row 100 (WS): dec, A x 32, turn (32 blocks).

↙ Row 101 (RS): dec, A x 31, turn (31 blocks).

↗ Row 102 (WS): dec, A x 30, turn (30 blocks).

↙ Row 103 (RS): dec, A x 29, turn (29 blocks).

↗ Row 104 (WS): dec, A x 28, turn (28 blocks).

↙ Row 105 (RS): dec, A x 27, turn (27 blocks).

↗ Row 106 (WS): dec, A x 26, turn (26 blocks).

↙ Row 107 (RS): dec, A x 25, turn (25 blocks).

↗ Row 108 (WS): dec, A x 24, turn (24 blocks).

↙ Row 109 (RS): dec, A x 23, turn (23 blocks).

↗ Row 110 (WS): dec, A x 22, turn (22 blocks).

↙ Row 111 (RS): dec, A x 21, turn (21 blocks).

↗ Row 112 (WS): dec, A x 20, turn (20 blocks).

↙ Row 113 (RS): dec, A x 19, turn (19 blocks).

↗ Row 114 (WS): dec, A x 18, turn (18 blocks).

↙ Row 115 (RS): dec, A x 17, turn (17 blocks).

↗ Row 116 (WS): dec, A x 16, turn (16 blocks).

↙ Row 117 (RS): dec, A x 15, turn (15 blocks).

↗ Row 118 (WS): dec, A x 14, turn (14 blocks).

↙ Row 119 (RS): dec, A x 13, turn (13 blocks).

↗ Row 120 (WS): dec, A x 12, turn (12 blocks).

↙ Row 121 (RS): dec, A x 11, turn (11 blocks).

↗ Row 122 (WS): dec, A x 10, turn (10 blocks).

↙ Row 123 (RS): dec, A x 9, turn (9 blocks).

↗ Row 124 (WS): dec, A x 8, turn (8 blocks).

↙ Row 125 (RS): dec, A x 7, turn (7 blocks).

↗ Row 126 (WS): dec, A x 6, turn (6 blocks).

↙ Row 127 (RS): dec, A x 5, turn (5 blocks).

↗ Row 128 (WS): dec, A x 4, turn (4 blocks).

↙ Row 129 (RS): dec, A x 3, turn (3 blocks).

↗ Row 130 (WS): dec, A x 2, turn (2 blocks).

↙ Row 131 (RS): dec, A x 1, fasten off yarn A (1 block).

Sew in all loose ends on WS of work.

Patchwork Half Squares

Create a throw using squares worked in two colours that are joined together as you go. This is a great design for using up leftover yarns from other projects and can be adjusted to any size you wish. If you would like a larger throw, use the yarn requirements for one square to calculate how much extra yarn you'll need.

SKILL LEVEL

◻◻◻

HOOK SIZE

4mm (US G-6)

BLOCK STITCH

3 tr block: (3 ch, 3 tr in ch sp)

TECHNIQUES

Join-as-you-go (see page 21)

SQUARE SIZE

15 x 15cm (6 x 6in)

THROW SIZE

91 x 122cm (36 x 48in)

YARN

Cascade 220 Superwash® (DK/8-ply/light worsted; 100g/3½oz; 100m/220yd)

🟧	A	287 Deep Sea Coral – 2 balls
🟩	B	288 Green Spruce – 2 balls
🟨	C	820 Lemon – 2 balls
🟥	D	827 Coral – 2 balls
🟨	E	851 Lime – 2 balls
🟪	F	1940 Peach – 2 balls
🟦	G	1942 Mint – 2 balls
🟦	H	1973 Seafoam Heather – 2 balls

Yarn per square

First colour: 18m (20yd)
Second colour: 15m (16yd)

ABBREVIATIONS & STITCHES

ch	chain
ch sp	chain space
dec	sl st in next 3 sts, sl st into 3-ch sp
inc	ch 6, 1 tr in fourth ch from hook, 1 tr in next 2 ch, sl st into ch sp of next block
rep	repeat
RS	right side
sl st	slip stitch
st(s)	stitch(es)
tr	treble crochet
WS	wrong side
↙/↗	direction of work

SQUARE LAYOUT CHART

Square

Make 48 squares

↙ **Row 1 (RS):** using yarn A, ch 6, 1 tr in fourth ch from hook, 1 tr in next 2 ch (1 block).

↗ **Row 2 (WS):** inc, A x 1, turn (2 blocks).

↙ **Row 3 (RS):** inc, A x 2, turn (3 blocks).

↗ **Row 4 (WS):** inc, A x 3, turn (4 blocks).

↙ **Row 5 (RS):** inc, A x 4, turn (5 blocks).

↗ **Row 6 (WS):** inc, A x 5, turn (6 blocks).

↙ **Row 7 (RS):** inc, A x 6, turn (7 blocks).

↗ **Row 8 (WS):** inc, A x 7, fasten off yarn A, turn (8 blocks).

Corner: start decreasing at both ends.

↙ **Row 9 (RS):** join yarn B in ch sp of last block made, B x 7, turn (7 blocks).

↗ **Row 10 (WS):** dec, B x 6, turn (6 blocks).

↙ **Row 11 (RS):** dec, B x 5, turn (5 blocks).

↗ **Row 12 (WS):** dec, B x 4, turn (4 blocks).

↙ **Row 13 (RS):** dec, B x 3, turn (3 blocks).

↗ **Row 14 (WS):** dec, B x 2, turn (2 blocks).

↙ **Row 15 (RS):** dec, B x 1, turn (1 block).

Sew in all loose ends on WS of work.

Repeat instructions above while joining as you go. Use random colours for each square or follow the colours used in the layout chart, aiming to use each colour fairly evenly.

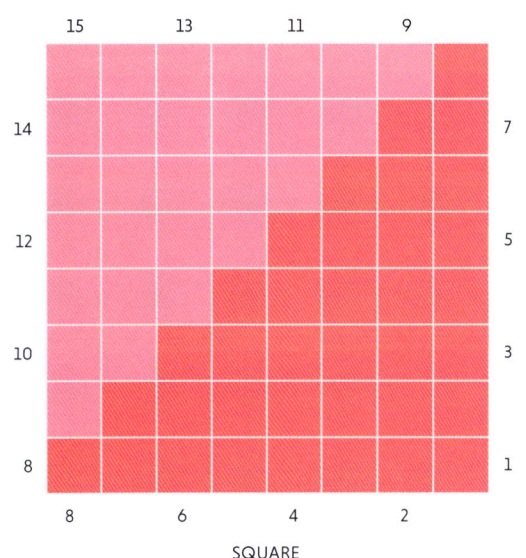

SQUARE

Patchwork Heart

Another great project for scrap-busting!
You can work each colour section of the heart
in a different colour to use up leftovers.

SKILL LEVEL

☐ ☐ ☐

HOOK SIZE

6mm (US J-10)

BLOCK STITCH

3 tr block: (3 ch, 3 tr in ch sp)

THROW SIZE

99 x 142cm (39 x 56in)

YARN

Cascade 220® (aran/10-ply/worsted;
100g/3½oz; 200m/220yd)

☐	**A**	8505 White – 8 balls
☐	**B**	1055 Jacaranda – 1 ball
☐	**C**	1072 Key West – 1 ball
☐	**D**	1070 Golden Kiwi – 1 ball
☐	**E**	9682 Desert Flower – 1 ball
☐	**F**	1057 Peony – 1 ball

Number of bobbins

B x 8, C x 8, D x 8, E x 7, F x 7

ABBREVIATIONS & STITCHES

ch	chain
ch sp	chain space
dec	sl st in next 3 sts, sl st into 3-ch sp
inc	ch 6, 1 tr in fourth ch from hook, 1 tr in next 2 ch, sl st into ch sp of next block
NB	join in new bobbin
RB	remove bobbin and cut yarn
rep	repeat
RS	right side
sl st	slip stitch
st(s)	stitch(es)
tr	treble crochet
WS	wrong side
↙/↗	direction of work

Throw

↙ Row 1 (RS): using yarn A, ch 6, 1 tr in fourth ch from hook, 1 tr in next 2 ch, turn (1 block).

↗ Row 2 (WS): inc, A x 1, turn (2 blocks).

↙ Row 3 (RS): inc, A x 2, turn (3 blocks).

↗ Row 4 (WS): inc, A x 3, turn (4 blocks).

↙ Row 5 (RS): inc, A x 4, turn (5 blocks).

↗ Row 6 (WS): inc, A x 5, turn (6 blocks).

↙ Row 7 (RS): inc, A x 6, turn (7 blocks).

↗ Row 8 (WS): inc, A x 7, turn (8 blocks).

↙ Row 9 (RS): inc, A x 8, turn (9 blocks).

↗ Row 10 (WS): inc, A x 9, turn (10 blocks).

↙ Row 11 (RS): inc, A x 10, turn (11 blocks).

↗ Row 12 (WS): inc, A x 11, turn (12 blocks).

↙ Row 13 (RS): inc, A x 12, turn (13 blocks).

↗ Row 14 (WS): inc, A x 13, turn (14 blocks).

↙ Row 15 (RS): inc, A x 14, turn (15 blocks).

↗ Row 16 (WS): inc, A x 15, turn (16 blocks).

↙ Row 17 (RS): inc, A x 16, turn (17 blocks).

↗ Row 18 (WS): inc, A x 17, turn (18 blocks).

↙ Row 19 (RS): inc, A x 18, turn (19 blocks).

↗ Row 20 (WS): inc, A x 19, turn (20 blocks).

↙ Row 21 (RS): inc, A x 20, turn (21 blocks).

↗ Row 22 (WS): inc, A x 21, turn (22 blocks).

↙ Row 23 (RS): inc, A x 22, turn (23 blocks).

↗ Row 24 (WS): inc, A x 23, turn (24 blocks).

↙ Row 25 (RS): inc, A x 24, turn (25 blocks).

↗ Row 26 (WS): inc, A x 25, turn (26 blocks).

↙ Row 27 (RS): inc, A x 26, turn (27 blocks).

↗ Row 28 (WS): inc, A x 27, turn (28 blocks).

↙ Row 29 (RS): inc, A x 28, turn (29 blocks).

↗ Row 30 (WS): inc, A x 29, turn (30 blocks).

↙ Row 31 (RS): inc, A x 30, turn (31 blocks).

↗ Row 32 (WS): inc, A x 31, turn (32 blocks).

↙ Row 33 (RS): inc, A x 32, turn (33 blocks).

↗ Row 34 (WS): inc, A x 33, turn (34 blocks).

↙ Row 35 (RS): inc, A x 34, turn (35 blocks).

↗ Row 36 (WS): inc, A x 35, turn (36 blocks).

↙ Row 37 (RS): inc, A x 36, turn (37 blocks).

↗ Row 38 (WS): inc, A x 37, turn (38 blocks).

↙ Row 39 (RS): inc, A x 38, turn (39 blocks).

↗ Row 40 (WS): inc, A x 39, turn (40 blocks).

↙ Row 41 (RS): inc, A x 40, turn (41 blocks).

↗ Row 42 (WS): inc, A x 41, turn (42 blocks).

↙ Row 43 (RS): inc, A x 42, turn (43 blocks).

↗ Row 44 (WS): inc, A x 43, turn (44 blocks).

↙ Row 45 (RS): inc, A x 44, turn (45 blocks).

↗ Row 46 (WS): inc, A x 45, turn (46 blocks).

↙ Row 47 (RS): inc, A x 46, turn (47 blocks).

↗ **Row 48 (WS):** inc, A x 47, turn (48 blocks).

Corner: start decreasing on WS.

↙ **Row 49 (RS):** inc, A x 47, turn (48 blocks).

↗ **Row 50 (WS):** dec, A x 24, B x 6, C x 6, D x 6, with a new ball of yarn A x 6, turn (48 blocks).

↙ **Row 51 (RS):** inc, A x 5, E x 1, D x 5, B x 1, C x 5, D x 1, B x 5, C x 1, A x 23, turn (48 blocks).

↗ **Row 52 (WS):** dec, A x 23, C x 1, B x 4, D x 1, E x 1, C x 4, B x 1, F x 1, D x 4, E x 2, A x 6, turn (48 blocks).

↙ **Row 53 (RS):** inc, A x 5, E x 3, D x 3, F x 1, B x 2, C x 3, E x 1, D x 2, B x 3, C x 2, A x 22, turn (48 blocks).

↗ **Row 54 (WS):** dec, A x 22, C x 2, B x 2, D x 2, E x 2, C x 2, B x 2, F x 2, D x 2, E x 4, A x 6, turn (48 blocks).

↙ **Row 55 (RS):** inc, A x 5, E x 5, D x 1, fasten off yarn D, F x 2, B x 3, C x 1, fasten off yarn C, E x 2, D x 3, B x 1, fasten off yarn B, C x 3, A x 21, turn (48 blocks).

↗ **Row 56 (WS):** dec, A x 21, C x 3, D x 3, E x 3, B x 3, F x 3, E x 6, fasten off yarn E, A x 6, turn (48 blocks).

↙ **Row 57 (RS):** inc, A x 5, F x 1, C x 5, D x 1, F x 2, B x 3, F x 1, E x 2, D x 3, F x 1, C x 3, A x 20, turn (48 blocks).

↗ **Row 58 (WS):** dec, A x 20, C x 2, F x 2, D x 2, E x 2, F x 2, B x 2, F x 2, D x 2, C x 4, F x 1, A x 7, turn (48 blocks).

↙ **Row 59 (RS):** inc, A x 6, F x 2, C x 3, D x 3, F x 1, B x 2, F x 3, E x 1, D x 2, F x 3, C x 2, A x 19, turn (48 blocks).

↗ **Row 60 (WS):** dec, A x 19, C x 1, F x 4, D x 1, E x 1, fasten off yarn E, F x 4, B x 1, F x 1, fasten off yarn F, D x 4, C x 2, F x 2, A x 8, turn (48 blocks).

↙ **Row 61 (RS):** inc, A x 7, F x 3, C x 1, fasten off yarn C, D x 5, B x 1, fasten off yarn B, F x 5, D x 1, fasten off yarn D, F x 5, C x 1, fasten off yarn C, A x 18, turn (48 blocks).

↗ **Row 62 (WS):** dec, A x 18, F x 12, fasten off yarn F, D x 6, fasten off yarn D, F x 3, A x 9, turn (48 blocks).

↙ **Row 63 (RS):** inc, A x 8, F x 3, B x 1, C x 5, B x 1, E x 5, D x 1, C x 5, D x 1, A x 17, turn (48 blocks).

↗ **Row 64 (WS):** dec, A x 17, D x 1, C x 4, D x 2, E x 4, B x 2, C x 4, B x 2, F x 2, A x 10, turn (48 blocks).

↙ **Row 65 (RS):** inc, A x 9, F x 2, B x 3, C x 3, B x 3, E x 3, D x 3, C x 3, D x 2, A x 16, turn (48 blocks).

↗ **Row 66 (WS):** dec, A x 16, D x 2, C x 2, D x 4, E x 2, B x 4, C x 2, B x 4, F x 1, A x 11, turn (48 blocks).

↙ **Row 67 (RS):** inc, A x 10, F x 1, fasten off yarn F, B x 5, C x 1, fasten off yarn C, B x 5, E x 1, fasten off yarn E, D x 5, C x 1, fasten off yarn C, D x 3, A x 15, turn (48 blocks).

↗ **Row 68 (WS):** dec, A x 15, D x 9, B x 12, A x 12, turn (48 blocks).

↙ **Row 69 (RS):** inc, A x 12, F x 5, E x 1, D x 5, C x 1, B x 5, E x 1, D x 3, A x 14, turn (48 blocks).

Corner: start decreasing on WS.

↗ **Row 70 (WS):** dec, A x 14, D x 2, E x 2, B x 4, C x 2, D x 4, E x 2, F x 4, A x 13, turn (47 blocks).

↙ **Row 71 (RS):** dec, A x 13, F x 3, E x 3, D x 3, C x 3, B x 3, E x 3, D x 2, A x 13, turn (46 blocks).

↗ **Row 72 (WS):** dec, A x 13, D x 1, E x 4, B x yarn 2, C x 4, D x 2, E x 4, F x 2, A x 13, turn (45 blocks).

↙ **Row 73 (RS):** dec, A x 13, F x 1, fasten off yarn F, E x 5, D x 1, fasten off yarn D, C x 5, B x 1, fasten off yarn B, E x 5, D x 1, fasten off yarn D, A x 12, turn (44 blocks).

↗ **Row 74 (WS):** dec, A x 12, E x 6, fasten off yarn E, C x 6, E x 6, fasten off yarn E, A x 13, turn (43 blocks).

↙ **Row 75 (RS):** dec, A x 18, B x 1, D x 5, F x 1, B x 5, F x 1, A x 11, turn (42 blocks).

↗ **Row 76 (WS):** dec, A x 11, F x 1, B x 4, F x 2, D x 4, B x 1, A x 18, turn (41 blocks).

↙ **Row 77 (RS):** dec, A x 17, B x 2, D x 3, F x 3, B x 3, F x 2, A x 10, turn (40 blocks).

↗ **Row 78 (WS):** dec, A x 10, F x 2, B x 2, F x 4, D x 2, B x 2, A x 17, turn (39 blocks).

↙ **Row 79 (RS):** dec, A x 16, B x 3, D x 1, fasten off yarn D, F x 5, B x 1, F x 3, A x 9, turn (38 blocks).

↗ **Row 80 (WS):** dec, A x 9, F x 9, fasten off yarn F, B x 3, A x 16, turn (37 blocks).

↙ **Row 81 (RS):** dec, A x 15, B x 3, E x 1, C x 5, E x 1, F x 3, A x 8, turn (36 blocks).

↗ **Row 82 (WS):** dec, A x 8, F x 2, E x 2, C x 4, E x 1, C x 1, B x 2, A x 15, turn (35 blocks).

↙ **Row 83 (RS):** dec, A x 14, B x 2, C x 1, E x 2, C x 3, E x 3, F x 2, A x 7, turn (34 blocks).

↗ **Row 84 (WS):** dec, A x 7, F x 1, E x 4, C x 2, E x 2, C x 2, B x 1, A x 14, turn (33 blocks).

↙ **Row 85 (RS):** dec, A x 13, B x 1, fasten off yarn B, C x 2, E x 3, C x 1, fasten off yarn C, E x 5, fasten off yarn E, F x 1, fasten off yarn F, A x 6, turn (32 blocks).

↗ **Row 86 (WS):** dec, A x 6, E x 9, C x 3, A x 13, turn (31 blocks).

↙ **Row 87 (RS):** dec, A x 13, C x 2, E x 3, D x 1, B x 5, A x 6, turn (30 blocks).

↗ **Row 88 (WS):** dec, A x 6, B x 4, D x 2, E x 2, C x 2, A x 13, turn (29 blocks).

↙ **Row 89 (RS):** dec, A x 13, C x 1, E x 2, D x 3, B x 3, A x 6, turn (28 blocks).

↗ **Row 90 (WS):** dec, A x 6, B x 2, D x 4, E x 1, C x 1, fasten off yarn C, A x 13, turn (27 blocks).

↙ **Row 91 (RS):** dec, A x 13, E x 1, fasten off yarn E, D x 5, B x 1, fasten off yarn B, A x 6, turn (26 blocks).

↗ **Row 92 (WS):** dec, A x 6, D x 6, fasten off yarn D, A x 13, turn (25 blocks).

↙ **Row 93 (RS):** dec, A x 24, turn (24 blocks).

↙ **Row 94 (WS):** dec, A x 23, turn (23 blocks).

↙ **Row 95 (RS):** dec, A x 22, turn (22 blocks).

↗ **Row 96 (WS):** dec, A x 21, turn (21 blocks).

↙ **Row 97 (RS):** dec, A x 20, turn (20 blocks).

↗ **Row 98 (WS):** dec, A x 19, turn (19 blocks).

↙ **Row 99 (RS):** dec, A x 18, turn (18 blocks).

↙ **Row 100 (WS):** dec, A x 17, turn (17 blocks).

↙ **Row 101 (RS):** dec, A x 16, turn (16 blocks).

↗ **Row 102 (WS):** dec, A x 15, turn (15 blocks).

↙ **Row 103 (RS):** dec, A x 14, turn (14 blocks).

↗ **Row 104 (WS):** dec, A x 13, turn (13 blocks).

↙ **Row 105 (RS):** dec, A x 12, turn (12 blocks).

↗ **Row 106 (WS):** dec, A x 11, turn (11 blocks).

↙ **Row 107 (RS):** dec, A x 10, turn (10 blocks).

↗ **Row 108 (WS):** dec, A x 9, turn (9 blocks).

↙ **Row 109 (RS):** dec, A x 8, turn (8 blocks).

↗ **Row 110 (WS):** dec, A x 7, turn (7 blocks).

↙ **Row 111 (RS):** dec, A x 6, turn (6 blocks).

↗ **Row 112 (WS):** dec, A x 5, turn (5 blocks).

↙ **Row 113 (RS):** dec, A x 4, turn (4 blocks).

↙ **Row 114 (WS):** dec, A x 3, turn (3 blocks).

↙ **Row 115 (RS):** dec, A x 2, turn (2 blocks).

↗ **Row 116 (WS):** dec, A x 1, fasten off yarn A (1 block).

Sew in all loose ends on WS of work.

Triangles

If you have leftover yarns, you could try working each triangle in a different colour. For a larger blanket, you could work this up in an aran (worsted) weight yarn instead.

SKILL LEVEL

☐ ☐ ☐

HOOK SIZE

5mm (US H-8)

BLOCK STITCH

3 tr block: (3 ch, 3 tr in ch sp)

THROW SIZE

82 x 117cm (32¼ x 46in)

YARN

Cascade 220 Superwash® (DK/8-ply/ light worsted; 100g/3½oz; 200m/220yd)

- **A** 1942 Mint – 2 balls
- **B** 259 Blue Turquoise – 2 balls
- **C** 815 Black – 2 balls
- **D** 871 White – 2 balls
- **E** 874 Ridge Rock – 2 balls
- **F** 1973 Seafoam Heather – 2 balls

ABBREVIATIONS & STITCHES

ch	chain
ch sp	chain space
dec	sl st in next 3 sts, sl st into 3-ch sp
inc	ch 6, 1 tr in fourth ch from hook, 1 tr in next 2 ch, sl st into ch sp of next block
rep	repeat
RS	right side
sl st	slip stitch
st(s)	stitch(es)
tr	treble crochet
WS	wrong side
↙/↗	direction of work

NOTE

Carry unused colours under stitches.

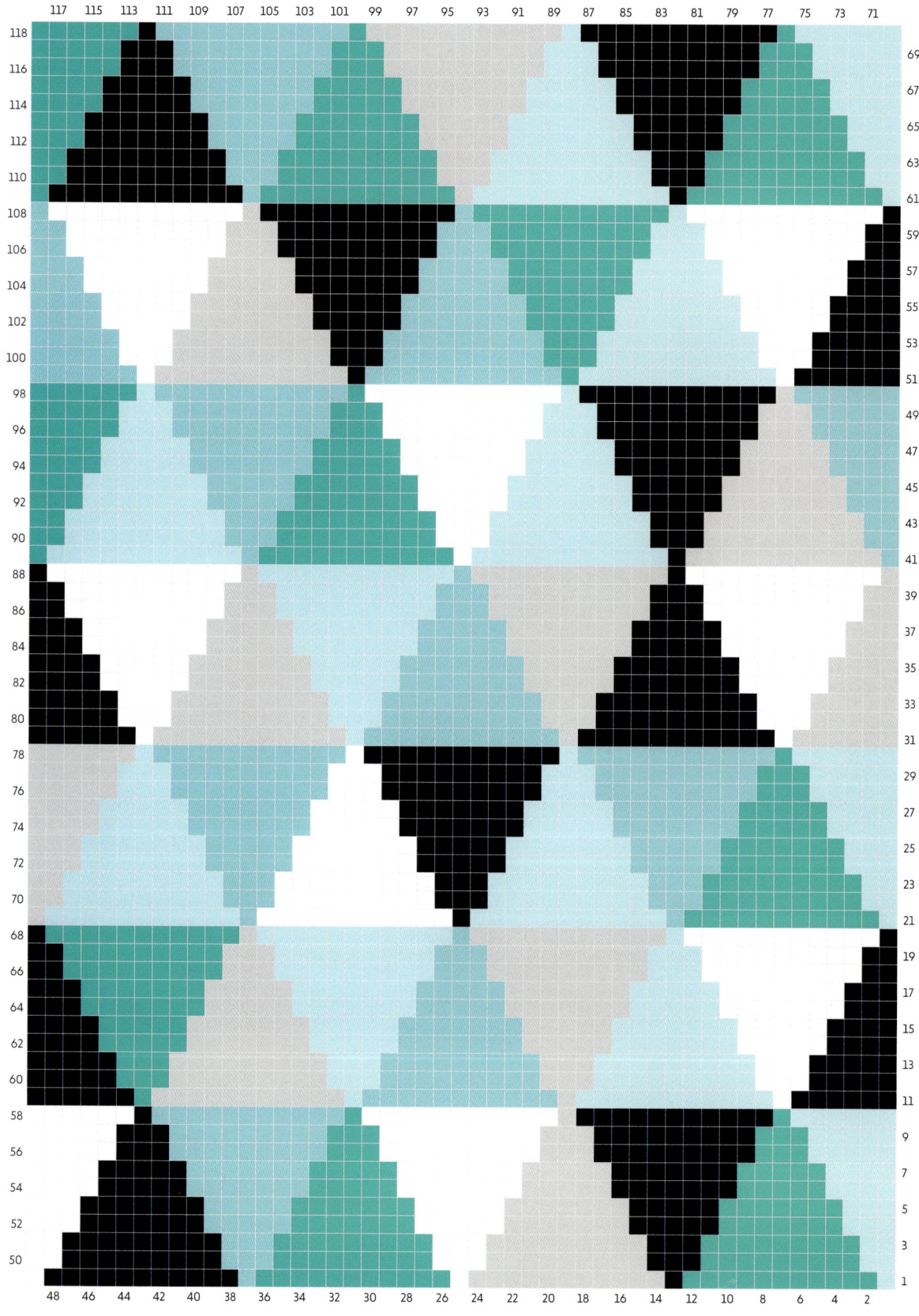

Throw

↙ Row 1 (RS): using yarn A, ch 6, 1 tr in third ch from hook and in next 2 ch, changing to yarn B when working last st, turn (1 block).

↗ Row 2 (WS): inc in B, A x 1, turn (2 blocks).

↙ Row 3 (RS): inc, A x 1, B x 1, turn (3 blocks).

↗ Row 4 (WS): inc, B x 1, A x 2, turn (4 blocks).

↙ Row 5 (RS): inc, A x 1, B x 3, turn (5 blocks).

↗ Row 6 (WS): inc, B x 2, A x 3, turn (6 blocks).

↙ Row 7 (RS): inc, A x 2, B x 4, turn (7 blocks).

↗ Row 8 (WS): inc, B x 4, A x 3, turn (8 blocks).

↙ Row 9 (RS): inc, A x 3, B x 5, turn (9 blocks).

↗ Row 10 (WS): inc, B x 5, A x 4, changing to yarn C when working last st, turn (10 blocks).

↙ Row 11 (RS): inc in C, A x 3, B x 7, turn (11 blocks).

↗ Row 12 (WS): inc, B x 6, A x 3, C x 2, turn (12 blocks).

↙ Row 13 (RS): inc, C x 2, A x 2, B x 6, C x 2, changing to yarn E when working last st, turn (13 blocks).

↗ Row 14 (WS): inc in E, C x 3, B x 5, A x 1, C x 4, turn (14 blocks).

↙ Row 15 (RS): inc, C x 4, A x 1, fasten off yarn A, B x 3, C x 5, E x 1, turn (15 blocks).

↗ Row 16 (WS): inc, E x 1, C x 6, B x 2, fasten off yarn B, C x 6, turn (16 blocks).

↙ Row 17 (RS): inc, C x 4, D x 2, C x 7, E x 3, turn (17 blocks).

↗ Row 18 (WS): inc, E x 2, C x 7, A x 1, D x 3, C x 4, turn (18 blocks).

↙ Row 19 (RS): inc, C x 2, D x 5, A x 1, C x 6, E x 4, turn (19 blocks).

↗ Row 20 (WS): inc, E x 4, C x 5, A x 2, D x 6, C x 2, changing to yarn A when working last st, fasten off yarn C, turn (20 blocks).

↙ Row 21 (RS): inc in A, D x 7, A x 3, C x 5, E x 5, turn (21 blocks).

↗ Row 22 (WS): inc, E x 5, C x 4, A x 3, D x 7, B x 1, A x 1, turn (22 blocks).

↙ Row 23 (RS): inc, A x 1, B x 1, D x 6, A x 4, C x 3, E x 7, turn (23 blocks).

↗ Row 24 (WS): inc, E x 6, C x 3, A x 5, D x 5, B x 2, A x 2, turn (24 blocks).

↙ Row 25 (RS): inc, A x 1, B x 3, D x 5, A x 5, C x 2, E x 6, D x 2 changing to yarn B when working last st, turn (25 blocks).

↗ Row 26 (WS): inc in B, D x 3, E x 5, C x 1, A x 6, D x 4, B x 3, A x 3, turn (26 blocks).

↙ Row 27 (RS): inc, A x 2, B x 4, D x 3, A x 7, C x 1, fasten off yarn C, E x 3, D x 5, B x 1, turn (27 blocks).

↗ Row 28 (WS): inc, B x 1, D x 6, E x 2, A x 7, D x 3, B x 5, A x 3, turn (28 blocks).

↙ Row 29 (RS): inc, A x 3, B x 5, D x 2, A x 6, E x 2, D x 7, B x 3, turn (29 blocks).

↗ Row 30 (WS): inc, B x 2, D x 7, F x 1, E x 3, A x 5, D x 1, B x 6, A x 4 changing to yarn E when working last st, turn (30 blocks).

↙ Row 31 (RS): inc in E, A x 3, B x 7, D x 1, fasten off yarn D, A x 3, E x 5, F x 1, D x 6, B x 4, turn (31 blocks).

↗ Row 32 (WS): inc, B x 4, D x 5, F x 2, E x 6, A x 2, fasten off yarn A, B x 7, A x 3, E x 2, turn (32 blocks).

↙ Row 33 (RS): inc, E x 2, A x 2, B x 6, F x 2, E x 7, F x 3, D x 5, B x 5, turn (33 blocks).

↗ Row 34 (WS): inc, B x 5, D x 4, F x 3, E x 7, A x 1, F x 3, B x 5, A x 1, E x 4, turn (34 blocks).

↙ Row 35 (RS): inc, E x 4, A x 1, fasten off yarn A, B x 3, F x 5, A x 1, E x 6, F x 4, D x 3, B x 7, turn (35 blocks).

↗ Row 36 (WS): inc, B x 6, D x 3, F x 5, E x 5, A x 2, F x 6, B x 2, fasten off yarn B, E x 6, turn (36 blocks).

↙ Row 37 (RS): inc, E x 4, D x 2, F x 7, A x 3, E x 5, F x 5, D x 2, B x 6, F x 2 changing to yarn C when working last st, turn (37 blocks).

↗ Row 38 (WS): inc in C, F x 3, B x 5, D x 1, F x 6, E x 4, A x 3, F x 7, C x 1, D x 3, E x 4, turn (38 blocks).

↙ **Row 39 (RS):** inc, E x 2, D x 5, C x 1, F x 6, A x 4, E x 3, F x 7, D x 1, fasten off yarn D, B x 3, F x 5, C x 1, turn (39 blocks).

↗ **Row 40 (WS):** inc, C x 1, F x 6, B x 2, F x 7, E x 3, A x 5, F x 5, C x 2, D x 6, E x 2 changing to yarn F when working last st, fasten off yarn E, turn (40 blocks).

↙ **Row 41 (RS):** inc in F, D x 7, C x 3, F x 5, A x 5, E x 2, F x 6, A x 2, F x 7, C x 3, turn (41 blocks).

↗ **Row 42 (WS):** inc, C x 2, F x 7, E x 1, A x 3, F x 5, E x 1, A x 6, F x 4, C x 3, D x 7, E x 1, F x 1, turn (42 blocks).

↙ **Row 43 (RS):** inc, F x 1, E x 1, D x 6, C x 4, F x 3, A x 7, E x 1, F x 3, A x 5, E x 1, F x 6, C x 4, turn (43 blocks).

↗ **Row 44 (WS):** inc, C x 4, F x 5, E x 2, A x 6, F x 2, A x 7, F x 3, C x 5, D x 5, E x 2, F x 2, turn (44 blocks).

↙ **Row 45 (RS):** inc, F x 1, E x 3, D x 5, C x 5, F x 2, A x 6, C x 2, fasten off yarn C, A x 7, E x 3, F x 5, C x 5, turn (45 blocks).

↗ **Row 46 (WS):** inc, C x 5, F x 4, E x 3, A x 7, D x 1, C x 3, A x 5, F x 1, C x 6, D x 4, E x 3, F x 3, turn (46 blocks).

↙ **Row 47 (RS):** inc, F x 2, E x 4, D x 3, C x 7, F x 1, fasten off yarn F, A x 3, C x 5, D x 1, A x 6, E x 4, F x 3, C x 7, turn (47 blocks).

↗ **Row 48 (WS):** inc, C x 6, F x 3, E x 5, A x 5, D x 2, fasten off yarn D, C x 6, A x 2, C x 7, D x 3, E x 5, F x 3, turn (48 blocks).

↙ **Row 49 (RS):** inc, F x 3, E x 5, D x 2, C x 6, E x 2, C x 7, D x 3, A x 5, E x 5, F x 2, C x 6, D x 2, turn (49 blocks).

Corner: start decreasing on WS.

↗ **Row 50 (WS):** dec, D x 3, C x 5, F x 1, E x 6, A x 4, D x 3, C x 7, F x 1, E x 3, C x 5, D x 1, E x 6, F x 4 changing to yarn C when working last st, turn (49 blocks).

↙ **Row 51 (RS):** inc in C, F x 3, E x 7, D x 1, fasten off yarn D, C x 3, E x 5, F x 1, fasten off yarn F, C x 6, D x 4, A x 3, E x 7, F x 1, C x 3, D x 4, turn (49 blocks).

↗ **Row 52 (WS):** dec, D x 5, C x 2, fasten off yarn C, E x 7, A x 3, D x 5, C x 5, F x 2, E x 6, C x 2, E x 7, F x 3, C x 2, turn (49 blocks).

↙ **Row 53 (RS):** inc, C x 2, F x 2, E x 6, C x 2, E x 7, F x 3, C x 5, D x 5, A x 2, E x 6, B x 2, D x 6, turn (49 blocks).

↗ **Row 54 (WS):** dec, D x 5, C x 1, B x 3, E x 5, A x 1, D x 6, C x 4, F x 3, E x 7, A x 1, C x 3, E x 5, F x 1, C x 4, turn (49 blocks).

↙ **Row 55 (RS):** inc, C x 4, F x 1, fasten off yarn F, E x 3, C x 5, A x 1, E x 6, F x 4, C x 3, D x 7, A x 1, E x 3, B x 5, C x 1, D x 4, turn (49 blocks).

↗ **Row 56 (WS):** dec, D x 2, C x 2, B x 6, E x 2, fasten off yarn E, D x 7, C x 3, F x 5, E x 5, A x 2, C x 6, E x 2, C x 6, turn (49 blocks).

↙ **Row 57 (RS):** inc, C x 4, D x 2, C x 7, A x 3, E x 5, F x 5, C x 2, D x 6, F x 2, B x 7, C x 3, D x 2, turn (49 blocks).

↗ **Row 58 (WS):** dec, D x 1, C x 3, B x 7, A x 1, F x 3, D x 5, C x 1, F x 6, E x 4, A x 3, C x 7, A x 1, D x 3, C x 4, turn (49 blocks).

↙ **Row 59 (RS):** inc, C x 2, D x 5, A x 1, C x 6, A x 4, E x 3, F x 7, C x 1, fasten off yarn C, D x 3, F x 5, A x 1, B x 6, C x 4, turn (49 blocks).

↗ **Row 60 (WS):** dec, C x 4, B x 5, A x 2, F x 6, D x 2, fasten off yarn D, F x 7, E x 3, A x 5, C x 5, A x 2, D x 6, C x 2 changing to yarn A when working last st, fasten off yarn C, turn (49 blocks).

↙ **Row 61 (RS):** inc in A, D x 7, A x 3, C x 5, A x 5, E x 2, F x 6, A x 2, F x 7, A x 3, B x 5, C x 3, turn (49 blocks).

↗ Row 62 (WS): dec, C x 3, B x 4, A x 3, F x 7, E x 1, A x 3, F x 5, E x 1, A x 6, C x 4, A x 3, D x 7, B x 1, A x 1, turn (49 blocks).

↙ Row 63 (RS): inc, A x 1, B x 1, D x 6, A x 4, C x 3, A x 7, E x 1, fasten off yarn E, F x 3, A x 5, E x 1, F x 6, A x 4, B x 3, C x 3, turn (49 blocks).

↗ Row 64 (WS): dec, C x 2, B x 3, A x 5, F x 5, E x 2, A x 6, F x 2, fasten off yarn F, A x 7, C x 3, A x 5, D x 5, B x 2, A x 2, turn (49 blocks).

↙ Row 65 (RS): inc, A x 1, B x 3, D x 5, A x 5, C x 2, A x 6, D x 2, A x 7, E x 3, F x 5, A x 5, B x 2, C x 2, turn (49 blocks).

↗ Row 66 (WS): dec, C x 2, B x 1, A x 6, F x 4, E x 3, A x 7, B x 1, D x 3, A x 5, C x 1, A x 6, D x 4, B x 3, A x 3, turn (49 blocks).

↙ Row 67 (RS): inc, A x 2, B x 4, D x 3, A x 7, C x 1, fasten off yarn C, A x 3, D x 5, B x 1, A x 6, E x 4, F x 3, A x 7, B x 1, fasten off yarn B, C x 1, turn (49 blocks).

↗ Row 68 (WS): dec, C x 1, fasten off yarn C, A x 7, F x 3, E x 5, A x 5, B x 2, D x 6, A x 9, D x 3, B x 5, A x 3, turn (49 blocks).

↙ Row 69 (RS): inc, A x 3, B x 5, D x 2, A x 6, B x 2, D x 7, B x 3, A x 5, E x 5, F x 2, A x 6, E x 2, turn (49 blocks).

↗ Row 70 (WS): dec, E x 3, A x 5, F x 1, E x 6, A x 4, B x 3, D x 7, F x 1, B x 3, A x 5, D x 1, B x 6, A x 4, turn (49 blocks).

Corner: start decreasing on RS.

↙ Row 71 (RS): dec, A x 3, B x 7, D x 1, fasten off yarn D, A x 3, B x 5, F x 1, fasten off yarn F, D x 6, B x 4, A x 3, X x 7, F x 1, A x 3, E x 4, turn (48 blocks).

↗ Row 72 (WS): dec, E x 5, A x 2, fasten off yarn A, E x 7, A x 3, B x 5, D x 5, F x 2, B x 6, A x 2, B x 7, A x 3, turn (47 blocks).

↙ Row 73 (RS): dec, A x 2, B x 6, C x 2, B x 7, F x 3, D x 5, B x 5, A x 2, E x 6, D x 2, E x 6, turn (46 blocks).

↗ Row 74 (WS): dec, E x 5, C x 1, D x 3, E x 5, A x 1, B x 6, D x 4, F x 3, B x 7, A x 1, C x 3, B x 5, A x 1, turn (45 blocks).

↙ Row 75 (RS): dec, A x 1, B x 3, C x 5, A x 1, fasten off yarn A, B x 6, F x 4, D x 3, B x 7, A x 1, E x 3, D x 5, C x 1, E x 4, turn (44 blocks).

↗ Row 76 (WS): dec, E x 3, C x 2, D x 6, E x 2, B x 7, D x 3, F x 5, B x 5, A x 2, C x 6, B x 2, fasten off yarn B, turn (43 blocks).

↙ Row 77 (RS): join yarn C in last ch sp made, C x 7, A x 3, B x 5, F x 5, D x 2, B x 6, F x 2, D x 7, C x 3, E x 2, turn (42 blocks).

↗ Row 78 (WS): dec, E x 1, fasten off yarn E, C x 3, D x 7, A x 1, F x 3, B x 5, D x 1, F x 6, B x 4, A x 3, C x 7, turn (41 blocks).

↙ Row 79 (RS): dec, C x 6, A x 4, B x 3, F x 7, D x 1, fasten off yarn D, B x 3, F x 5, A x 1, D x 6, C x 4, turn (40 blocks).

↗ Row 80 (WS): dec, C x 4, D x 5, A x 2, F x 6, B x 2, fasten off yarn B, F x 7, B x 3, A x 5, C x 5, turn (39 blocks).

↙ Row 81 (RS): dec, C x 5, A x 5, B x 2, F x 6, C x 2, F x 7, A x 3, D x 5, C x 3, turn (38 blocks).

↗ Row 82 (WS): dec, C x 3, D x 4, A x 3, F x 7, E x 1, C x 3, F x 5, B x 1, A x 6, C x 4, turn (37 blocks).

↙ Row 83 (RS): dec, C x 3, A x 7, B x 1, fasten off yarn B, F x 3, C x 5, E x 1, F x 6, A x 4, D x 3, C x 3, turn (36 blocks).

↗ Row 84 (WS): dec, C x 2, D x 3, A x 5, F x 5, E x 2, C x 6, F x 2, fasten off yarn F, A x 7, C x 3, turn (35 blocks).

↙ Row 85 (RS): dec, C x 2, A x 6, E x 2, C x 7, E x 3, F x 5, A x 5, D x 2, C x 2, turn (34 blocks).

↗ Row 86 (WS): dec, C x 2, D x 1, A x 6, F x 4, E x 3, C x 7, B x 1, E x 3, A x 5, C x 1, turn (33 blocks).

↙ Row 87 (RS): dec, C x 1, fasten off yarn C, A x 3, E x 5, B x 1, C x 6, E x 4, F x 3, A x 7, D x 1, fasten off yarn D, C x 1, turn (32 blocks).

↗ Row 88 (WS): dec, C x 1, fasten off yarn C, A x 7, F x 3, E x 5, C x 5, B x 2, E x 6, A x 2, fasten off yarn A, turn (31 blocks).

↙ Row 89 (RS): join yarn E in last ch sp made, E x 7, B x 3, C x 5, E x 5, F x 2, A x 6, B x 2, turn (30 blocks).

↗ Row 90 (WS): dec, B x 3, A x 5, F x 1, E x 6, C x 4, B x 3, E x 7, turn (29 blocks).

↙ Row 91 (RS): dec, E x 6, B x 4, C x 3, E x 7, F x 1, fasten off yarn F, A x 3, B x 4, turn (28 blocks).

↗ Row 92 (WS): dec, B x 5, A x 2, fasten off yarn A, E x 7, C x 3, B x 5, E x 5, turn (27 blocks).

↙ Row 93 (RS): dec, E x 5, B x 5, C x 2, E x 6, D x 2, B x 6, turn (26 blocks).

↗ Row 94 (WS): dec, B x 5, F x 1, D x 3, E x 5, C x 1, B x 6, E x 4, turn (25 blocks).

↙ Row 95 (RS): dec, E x 3, B x 7, C x 1, fasten off yarn C, E x 3, D x 5, F x 1, B x 4, turn (24 blocks).

↗ Row 96 (WS): dec, B x 3, F x 2, D x 6, E x 2, fasten off yarn E, B x 7, E x 3, turn (23 blocks).

↙ Row 97 (RS): dec, E x 2, B x 6, F x 2, D x 7, F x 3, B x 2, turn (22 blocks).

↗ Row 98 (WS): dec, B x 1, fasten off yarn B, F x 3, D x 7, C x 1, F x 3, B x 5, E x 1, turn (21 blocks).

↙ Row 99 (RS): dec, E x 1, fasten off yarn E, B x 3, F x 5, C x 1, D x 6, F x 4, turn (20 blocks).

↗ Row 100 (WS): dec, F x 4, D x 5, C x 2, F x 6, B x 2, fasten off yarn B, turn (19 blocks).

↙ Row 101 (RS): join yarn F in last ch sp, F x 7, C x 3, D x 5, F x 3, turn (18 blocks).

↗ Row 102 (WS): dec, F x 3, D x 4, C x 3, F x 7, turn (17 blocks).

↙ Row 103 (RS): dec, F x 6, C x 4, D x 3, F x 3, turn (16 blocks).

↗ Row 104 (WS): dec, F x 2, D x 3, C x 5, F x 5, turn (15 blocks).

↙ Row 105 (RS): dec, F x 5, C x 5, D x 2, F x 2, turn (14 blocks).

↗ Row 106 (WS): dec, F x 2, D x 1, C x 6, F x 4, turn (13 blocks).

↙ Row 107 (RS): dec, F x 3, C x 7, D x 1, fasten off yarn D, F x 1, fasten off yarn D, turn (12 blocks).

↗ Row 108 (WS): dec, F x 1, fasten off yarn F, C x 7, F x 3, turn (11 blocks).

↙ Row 109 (RS): dec, F x 2, C x 6, B x 2, turn (10 blocks).

↗ Row 110 (WS): dec, B x 3, C x 5, F x 1, turn (9 blocks).

↙ Row 111 (RS): dec, F x 1, fasten off yarn F, C x 3, B x 4, turn (8 blocks).

↗ Row 112 (WS): dec, B x 5, C x 2, fasten off yarn C, turn (7 blocks).

↙ Row 113 (RS): join yarn B in last ch sp, B x 6, turn (6 blocks).

↗ Row 114 (WS): dec, B x 5, turn (5 blocks).

↙ Row 115 (RS): dec, B x 4, turn (4 blocks).

↗ Row 116 (WS): dec, B x 3, turn (3 blocks).

↙ Row 117 (RS): dec, B x 2, turn (2 blocks).

↗ Row 118 (WS): dec, B x 1, fasten off yarn B (1 block).

Sew in all loose ends on WS of work.

Sweethearts

This throw is created with heart-patterned squares that are sewn together once complete, making it perfect for a loved one. You can also crochet the squares together if you prefer. If you would like a larger throw, use the yarn requirements for one square to calculate how much extra yarn you'll need.

SKILL LEVEL

■ ■ □

HOOK SIZE

4mm (US G-6)

BLOCK STITCH

3 tr block: (3 ch, 3 tr in ch sp)

TECHNIQUES

Join-as-you-go (see page 21)
Colour changes (see page 22)

SQUARE SIZE

30 x 30cm (12 x 12in)

THROW SIZE

90 x 120cm (35½ x 47¼in)

YARN

Cascade 220 Superwash® (DK/8-ply/light worsted; 100g/3½oz; 200m/220yd)

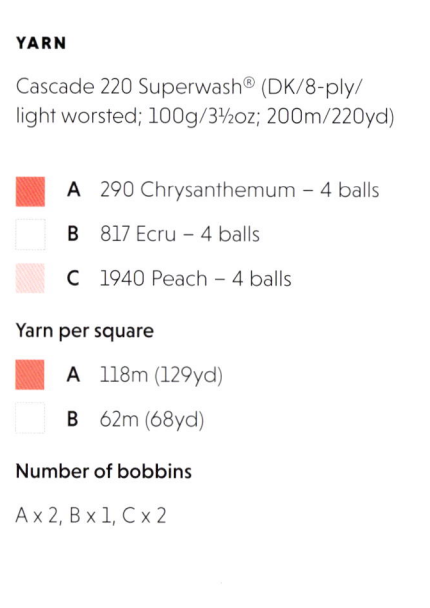

A   290 Chrysanthemum – 4 balls

B   817 Ecru – 4 balls

C   1940 Peach – 4 balls

Yarn per square

A   118m (129yd)

B   62m (68yd)

Number of bobbins

A x 2, B x 1, C x 2

ABBREVIATIONS & STITCHES

ch	chain
ch sp	chain space
dc	double crochet
dec	sl st in next 3 sts, sl st into 3-ch sp
inc	ch 6, 1 tr in fourth ch from hook, 1 tr in next 2 ch, sl st into ch sp of next block
NB	join in new bobbin
RB	remove bobbin and cut yarn
rep	repeat
RS	right side
sl st	slip stitch
st(s)	stitch(es)
tr	treble crochet
WS	wrong side
[ ]	repeat instructions between square brackets number of times stated
↙ / ↗	direction of work

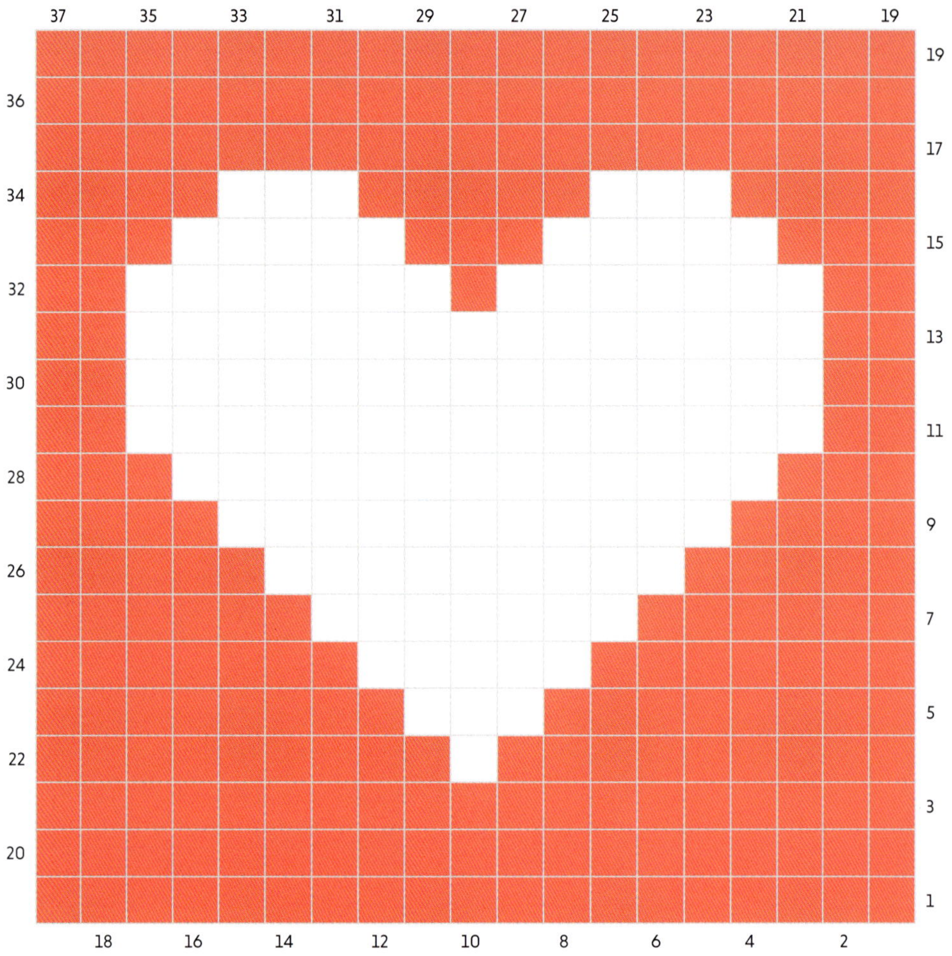

Top axis: 37 35 33 31 29 27 25 23 21 19

Right axis: 19 17 15 13 11 9 7 5 3 1

Left axis: 36 34 32 30 28 26 24 22 20

Bottom axis: 18 16 14 12 10 8 6 4 2

SQUARE

Square

Make 6 squares in each of 2 colourways:
yarn A and yarn B; yarn C and yarn B

↙ **Row 1 (RS):** using yarn A, ch 6, 1 tr in fourth ch from hook and in next 2 ch, turn (1 block).

↗ **Row 2 (WS):** inc, A x 1, turn (2 blocks).

↙ **Row 3 (RS):** inc, A x 2, turn (3 blocks).

↗ **Row 4 (WS):** inc, A x 3, turn (4 blocks).

↙ **Row 5 (RS):** inc, A x 4, turn (5 blocks).

↗ **Row 6 (WS):** inc, A x 5, turn (6 blocks).

↙ **Row 7 (RS):** inc, A x 6, turn (7 blocks).

↗ **Row 8 (WS):** inc, A x 7, turn (8 blocks).

↙ **Row 9 (RS):** inc, A x 8, turn (9 blocks).

↗ **Row 10 (WS):** inc, A x 9, turn (10 blocks).

↙ **Row 11 (RS):** inc, A x 10, turn (11 blocks).

↗ **Row 12 (WS):** inc, A x 11, turn (12 blocks).

↙ **Row 13 (RS):** inc, A x 1, B x 8, A x 3, turn (13 blocks).

↗ **Row 14 (WS):** inc, A x 3, B x 8, A x 2, turn (14 blocks).

↙ **Row 15 (RS):** inc, A x 1, B x 9, A x 4, turn (15 blocks).

↗ **Row 16 (WS):** inc, A x 4, B x 9, A x 2, turn (16 blocks).

↙ **Row 17 (RS):** inc, A x 2, B x 9, A x 5, turn (17 blocks).

↗ **Row 18 (WS):** inc, A x 5, B x 9, A x 3, turn (18 blocks).

↙ **Row 19 (RS):** inc, A x 3, B x 9, A x 6, turn (19 blocks).

Corner: start decreasing at both ends.

↗ **Row 20 (WS):** dec, A x 6, B x 9, A x 3, turn (18 blocks).

↙ **Row 21 (RS):** dec, A x 3, B x 9, A x 5, turn (17 blocks).

SQUARE LAYOUT CHART

Row 22 (WS): dec, A x 5, B x 8, A x 3, turn (16 blocks).

Row 23 (RS): dec, A x 6, B x 5, A x 4, turn (15 blocks).

Row 24 (WS): dec, A x 4, B x 5, A x 5, turn (14 blocks).

Row 25 (RS): dec, A x 5, B x 5, A x 3, turn (13 blocks).

Row 26 (WS): dec, A x 3, B x 5, A x 4, turn (12 blocks).

Row 27 (RS): dec, A x 4, B x 5, A x 2, turn (11 blocks).

Row 28 (WS): dec, A x 2, B x 5, A x 3, turn (10 blocks).

Row 29 (RS): dec, A x 3, B x 4, A x 2, turn (9 blocks).

Row 30 (WS): dec, A x 2, B x 3, A x 3, turn (8 blocks).

Row 31 (RS): dec, A x 7, turn (7 blocks).

Row 32 (WS): dec, A x 6, turn (6 blocks).

Row 33 (RS): dec, A x 5, turn (5 blocks).

Row 34 (WS): dec, A x 4, turn (4 blocks).

Row 35 (RS): dec, A x 3, turn (3 blocks).

Row 36 (WS): dec, A x 2, turn (2 blocks).

Row 37 (RS): dec, A x 1 (1 block).

Edging

Now work in the round and continue with yarn A.

Round 1 (RS): ch 1 (does not count as a st), 3 dc in top of same st, 1 dc in next 2 sts, [2 dc into ch sp of next block, 1 dc into each of next 3 sts of next block] nine times, 2 dc into ch sp of next block, 1 dc in next 2 sts of next block, 3 dc in last st of same block, now working along next edge, [2 dc into side of st of next block, 1 dc into base of next 3 sts of next block] nine times, 2 dc into side of st of next block, 3 dc in bottom of same st, now working along next edge, [1 dc in base of next 2 sts of next block, 2 dc in side of st of next block] nine times, 1 dc in base of next 2 sts of next block, 3 dc in base of next st of same block, now working along last edge, [2 dc into ch sp of next block, 1 dc in next 3 sts of next block] nine times, 2 dc in next ch sp of next block, join with sl st to first st made, fasten off. Sew in all loose ends on WS of work.

Joining

Sew squares together using the mattress stitch technique and yarn A. Follow the layout chart for the placing of squares.

Mulled Cider

This autumnal throw can be worked in any colour variation you want. Use separate balls of yarn for each colour section along the rows so you don't need to bother with bobbins.

SKILL LEVEL

HOOK SIZE

6mm (US J-10)

BLOCK STITCH

3 tr block: (3 ch, 3 tr in ch sp)

THROW SIZE

104 x 137cm (41 x 54in)

YARN

Cascade 220® (aran/10-ply/worsted; 100g/3½oz; 200m/220yd)

- **A** 4002 Jet – 2 balls
- **B** 1077 Oxblood Red – 2 balls
- **C** 2415 Sunflower – 2 balls
- **D** 9566 Olive Oil – 2 balls
- **E** 8415 Pear – 2 balls
- **F** 8010 Natural – 1 ball

ABBREVIATIONS & STITCHES

ch	chain
ch sp	chain space
dec	sl st in next 3 sts, sl st into 3-ch sp
inc	ch 6, 1 tr in fourth ch from hook, 1 tr in next 2 ch, sl st into ch sp of next block
RS	right side
sl st	slip stitch
st(s)	stitch(es)
tr	treble crochet
WS	wrong side
↙/↗	direction of work

Throw

↙ **Row 1 (RS):** using yarn A, 6 ch, 1 tr in fourth ch from hook, 1 tr in next 2 ch, turn (1 block).

↗ **Row 2 (WS):** inc in A, B x 1, turn (2 blocks).

↙ **Row 3 (RS):** inc, B x 1, A x 2, turn (3 blocks).

↗ **Row 4 (WS):** inc, A x 1, B x 2, turn (4 blocks).

↙ **Row 5 (RS):** inc, B x 1, A x 3, turn (5 blocks).

↗ **Row 6 (WS):** inc, A x 2, B x 3, turn (6 blocks).

↙ **Row 7 (RS):** inc, B x 2, A x 4, turn (7 blocks).

↗ **Row 8 (WS):** inc, A x 3, B x 4 changing to yarn C when working last st, turn (8 blocks).

↙ **Row 9 (RS):** inc in C, B x 3, A x 5, turn (9 blocks).

↗ **Row 10 (WS):** inc, A x 4, B x 4, C x 1, turn (10 blocks).

↙ **Row 11 (RS):** inc, C x 1, B x 3, A x 6, turn (11 blocks).

↗ **Row 12 (WS):** inc, A x 5, B x 4, fasten off yarn B, C x 2, turn (12 blocks).

↙ **Row 13 (RS):** inc, C x 2, join in yarn B, B x 3, A x 7, turn (13 blocks).

↗ **Row 14 (WS):** inc in A, B x 10, C x 3, turn (14 blocks).

↙ **Row 15 (RS):** inc, C x 3, B x 9, A x 2, turn (15 blocks).

↗ **Row 16 (WS):** inc, A x 1, B x 10, C x 3, D x 1, turn (16 blocks).

↙ **Row 17 (RS):** inc in D, C x 4, B x 9, A x 3, turn (17 blocks).

↗ **Row 18 (WS):** inc, A x 2, B x 10, C x 3, D x 2, turn (18 blocks).

↙ **Row 19 (RS):** inc, D x 1, C x 4, B x 9, A x 4, turn (19 blocks).

↗ **Row 20 (WS):** inc, A x 3, B x 10, fasten off yarn B, C x 3, D x 3, turn (20 blocks).

↙ **Row 21 (RS):** inc, D x 2, C x 10, B x 3, A x 5, turn (21 blocks).

↗ **Row 22 (WS):** inc, A x 4, B x 4, C x 9, D x 4 changing to yarn E when working last st, turn (22 blocks).

↙ **Row 23 (RS):** inc in E, D x 3, C x 10, B x 3, A x 6, turn (23 blocks).

↗ **Row 24 (WS):** inc, A x 5, B x 4, C x 9, D x 4, E x 1, turn (24 blocks).

↙ **Row 25 (RS):** inc, E x 1, D x 3, C x 10, B x 3, fasten off yarn B, A x 7, turn (25 blocks).

↗ **Row 26 (WS):** inc in A, B x 10, C x 9, D x 4, fasten off yarn D, E x 2, turn (26 blocks).

↙ **Row 27 (RS):** inc, E x 2, D x 3, C x 10, B x 9, A x 2, turn (27 blocks).

↗ Row 28 (WS): inc, A x 1, B x 10, C x 3, D x 10, E x 3, turn (28 blocks).

↙ Row 29 (RS): inc, E x 3, D x 9, C x 4, B x 9, A x 3, turn (29 blocks).

↗ Row 30 (WS): inc, A x 2, B x 10, C x 3, D x 10, E x 3, F x 1, turn (30 blocks).

↙ Row 31 (RS): inc in F, E x 4, D x 9, C x 4, B x 9, A x 4, turn (31 blocks).

↗ Row 32 (WS): inc, A x 3, B x 10, fasten off yarn B, C x 3, D x 10, E x 3, F x 2, turn (32 blocks).

↙ Row 33 (RS): inc, F x 1, E x 4, D x 9, C x 10, B x 3, A x 5, turn (33 blocks).

↗ Row 34 (WS): inc, A x 4, B x 4, C x 9, D x 10, fasten off yarn D, E x 3, fasten off yarn E, F x 3, fasten off yarn F, turn (34 blocks).

↙ Row 35 (RS): inc, E x 12, D x 3, C x 10, B x 3, A x 6, turn (35 blocks).

↗ Row 36 (WS): inc, A x 5, B x 4, C x 9, D x 4, E x 13, turn (36 blocks).

↙ Row 37 (RS): inc, E x 13, D x 3, C x 10, B x 3, fasten off yarn B, A x 7, turn (37 blocks).

↗ Row 38 (WS): inc in A, B x 10, C x 9, D x 4, E x 14, turn (38 blocks).

↙ Row 39 (RS): inc, E x 14, D x 3, fasten off yarn D, C x 10, B x 9, A x 2, turn (39 blocks).

↗ Row 40 (WS): inc, A x 1, B x 10, C x 3, D x 10, E x 15, turn (40 blocks).

↙ Row 41 (RS): inc, E x 15, D x 9, C x 4, B x 9, A x 3, turn (41 blocks).

↗ Row 42 (WS): inc, A x 2, B x 10, C x 3, D x 10, E x 3, F x 3, E x 3, D x 7, turn (42 blocks).

↙ Row 43 (RS): inc, D x 6, E x 4, F x 2, E x 4, D x 9, C x 4, B x 9, A x 4, turn (43 blocks).

↗ Row 44 (WS): inc, A x 3, B x 10, fasten off yarn B, C x 3, D x 10, E x 3, F x 3, E x 3, D x 8, turn (44 blocks).

↙ Row 45 (RS): inc, D x 7, E x 4, F x 2, E x 4, D x 9, C x 10, B x 3, A x 5, turn (45 blocks).

↗ Row 46 (WS): inc, A x 4, B x 4, C x 9, D x 10, fasten off yarn D, E x 3, F x 3, fasten off yarn F, E x 3, D x 9, turn (46 blocks).

↙ Row 47 (RS): inc, D x 8, E x 16, D x 3, C x 10, B x 3, A x 6, turn (47 blocks).

↗ Row 48 (WS): inc, A x 5, B x 4, C x 9, D x 4, E x 15, D x 10 changing to yarn C when working last st, fasten off yarn D, turn (48 blocks).

↙ Row 49 (RS): inc, C x 6, D x 3, E x 16, D x 3, C x 10, B x 3, fasten off yarn B, A x 7, fasten off yarn A, turn (49 blocks).

Corner: start decreasing on WS.

↗ Row 50 (WS): join yarn B in last ch sp made, B x 10, C x 9, D x 4, E x 15, D x 4, C x 7, turn (49 blocks).

↙ Row 51 (RS): inc, C x 7, D x 3, E x 16, D x 3, fasten off yarn D, C x 10, fasten off yarn C, B x 9, turn (49 blocks).

↗ Row 52 (WS): dec, B x 9, C x 3, D x 10, E x 15, D x 4, C x 8, turn (49 blocks).

↙ Row 53 (RS): inc, C x 8, D x 3, E x 16, D x 9, fasten off yarn D, C x 4, B x 8, turn (49 blocks).

↗ Row 54 (WS): dec, B x 8, C x 3, D x 10, E x 3, carry yarn E under sts, F x 3, E x 3, D x 10, C x 9, turn (49 blocks).

↙ Row 55 (RS): inc, C x 9, D x 9, E x 4, carry yarn E under sts, F x 2, E x 4, D x 9, C x 4, B x 7, turn (49 blocks).

↗ Row 56 (WS): dec, B x 7, fasten off yarn B, C x 3, D x 10, E x 3, carry yarn E under sts, F x 3, E x 3, D x 10, C x 3, B x 7, turn (49 blocks).

↙ Row 57 (RS): inc, B x 7, C x 4, D x 9, E x 4, F x 2, E x 4, D x 9, C x 10, turn (49 blocks).

↗ Row 58 (WS): dec, C x 9, D x 10, fasten off yarn D, E x 3, F x 3, E x 3, D x 10, C x 3, B x 8, turn (49 blocks).

↙ Row 59 (RS): inc, B x 7, C x 4, D x 9, E x 16, D x 3, C x 9, turn (49 blocks).

↗ Row 60 (WS): dec, C x 8, D x 4, E x 15, D x 10, fasten off yarn D, C x 3, B x 9, turn (49 blocks).

↙ Row 61 (RS): inc, B x 9, C x 10, D x 3, E x 16, D x 3, C x 8, turn (49 blocks).

↗ Row 62 (WS): dec, C x 7, D x 4, E x 15, D x 4, C x 9, B x 10 changing to yarn A when working last st, fasten off yarn B, turn (49 blocks).

↙ Row 63 (RS): inc, A x 6, B x 3, C x 10, D x 3, fasten off yarn D, E x 16, D x 3, C x 7, fasten off yarn C, turn (49 blocks).

Corner: start decreasing on RS.

↗ Row 64 (WS): join yarn D in last ch sp made, D x 10, E x 15, D x 4, C x 9, B x 4, A x 6, turn (48 blocks).

↙ Row 65 (RS): dec, A x 6, B x 3, C x 10, D x 3, fasten off yarn D, E x 16, D x 9, turn (47 blocks).

↗ Row 66 (WS): dec, D x 9, E x 3, F x 3, E x 3,

D x 10, C x 9, B x 4, A x 5, turn (46 blocks).

↙ Row 67 (RS): dec, A x 5, B x 3, fasten off yarn B, C x 10, D x 9, E x 4, F x 2, E x 4, D x 8, turn (45 blocks).

↗ Row 68 (WS): dec, D x 8, E x 3, F x 3, E x 3, D x 10, C x 3, B x 10, A x 4, turn (44 blocks).

↙ Row 69 (RS): dec, A x 4, B x 9, C x 4, D x 9, E x 4, F x 2, E x 4, D x 7, turn (43 blocks).

↗ Row 70 (WS): dec, D x 7, E x 3, F x 3, fasten off yarn F, E x 3, D x 10, fasten off yarn D, C x 3, B x 10, A x 3, turn (42 blocks).

↙ Row 71 (RS): dec, A x 3, B x 9, C x 4, D x 9, E x 16, turn (41 blocks).

↗ Row 72 (WS): dec, E x 15, D x 10, fasten off yarn D, C x 3, B x 10, A x 2, turn (40 blocks).

↙ Row 73 (RS): dec, A x 2, B x 9, C x 10, D x 3, E x 15, turn (39 blocks).

↗ Row 74 (WS): dec, E x 14, D x 4, C x 9, B x 10, fasten off yarn B, A x 1, turn (38 blocks).

↙ Row 75 (RS): dec, A x 7, B x 3, C x 10, D x 3, E x 14, turn (37 blocks).

↗ Row 76 (WS): dec, E x 13, D x 4, C x 9, B x 4, A x 6, turn (36 blocks).

↙ Row 77 (RS): dec, A x 6, B x 3, C x 10, D x 3, fasten off yarn D, E x 13, fasten off yarn E, turn (35 blocks).

↗ Row 78 (WS): join yarn F in last ch sp made, F x 3, E x 3, D x 10, C x 9, B x 4, A x 5, turn (34 blocks).

↙ Row 79 (RS): dec, A x 5, B x 3, fasten off yarn B, C x 10, D x 9, E x 4, F x 2, turn (33 blocks).

↗ Row 80 (WS): dec, F x 2, E x 3, D x 10, C x 3, B x 10, A x 4, turn (32 blocks).

↙ Row 81 (RS): dec, A x 4, B x 9, C x 4, D x 9, E x 4, F x 1, turn (31 blocks).

↗ Row 82 (WS): dec, F x 1, E x 3, D x 10, C x 3, B x 10, A x 3, turn (30 blocks).

↙ Row 83 (RS): dec, A x 3, B x 9, C x 4, D x 9, E x 4, turn (29 blocks).

↗ Row 84 (WS): dec, E x 3, D x 10, fasten off yarn D, C x 3, B x 10, A x 2, turn (28 blocks).

↙ Row 85 (RS): dec, A x 2, B x 9, C x 10, D x 3, E x 3, turn (27 blocks).

↗ Row 86 (WS): dec, E x 2, D x 4, C x 9, B x 10, fasten off yarn B, A x 1, turn (26 blocks).

↙ Row 87 (RS): dec, A x 7, B x 3, C x 10, D x 3, E x 2, turn (25 blocks).

↗ Row 88 (WS): dec, E x 1, D x 4, C x 9, B x 4, A x 6, turn (24 blocks).

↙ **Row 89 (RS):** dec, A x 6, B x 3, C x 10, D x 3, E x 1, fasten off yarn E, turn (23 blocks).

↗ **Row 90 (WS):** join yarn D in last ch sp made, D x 4, C x 9, B x 4, A x 5, turn (22 blocks).

↙ **Row 91 (RS):** dec, A x 5, B x 3, fasten off yarn B, C x 10, D x 3, turn (21 blocks).

↗ **Row 92 (WS):** dec, D x 3, C x 3, B x 10, A x 4, turn (20 blocks).

↙ **Row 93 (RS):** dec, A x 4, B x 9, C x 4, D x 2, turn (19 blocks).

↗ **Row 94 (WS):** dec, D x 2, C x 3, B x 10, A x 3, turn (18 blocks).

↙ **Row 95 (RS):** dec, A x 3, B x 9, C x 4, D x 1, turn (17 blocks).

↗ **Row 96 (WS):** dec, D x 1, fasten off yarn D, C x 3, B x 10, A x 2, turn (16 blocks).

↙ **Row 97 (RS):** dec, A x 2, B x 9, C x 4, turn (15 blocks).

↗ **Row 98 (WS):** dec, C x 3, B x 10, fasten off yarn B, A x 1, turn (14 blocks).

↙ **Row 99 (RS):** dec, A x 7, B x 3, C x 3, turn (13 blocks).

↗ **Row 100 (WS):** dec, C x 2, B x 4, A x 6, turn (12 blocks).

↙ **Row 101 (RS):** dec, A x 6, B x 3, C x 2, turn (11 blocks).

↗ **Row 102 (WS):** dec, C x 1, B x 4, A x 5, turn (10 blocks).

↙ **Row 103 (RS):** dec, A x 5, B x 3, C x 1, fasten off yarn C, turn (9 blocks).

↗ **Row 104 (WS):** join yarn B in last ch sp made, B x 4, A x 4, turn (8 blocks).

↙ **Row 105 (RS):** dec, A x 4, B x 3, turn (7 blocks).

↗ **Row 106 (WS):** dec, B x 3, A x 3, turn (6 blocks).

↙ **Row 107 (RS):** dec, A x 3, B x 2, turn (5 blocks).

↗ **Row 108 (WS):** dec, B x 2, A x 2, turn (4 blocks).

↙ **Row 109 (RS):** dec, A x 2, B x 1, turn (3 blocks).

↗ **Row 110 (WS):** dec, B x 1, A x 1, turn (2 blocks).

↙ **Row 111 (RS):** dec, A x 1, turn (1 block).

Sew in all loose ends on WS of work.

Rainbow Stripes

This elegant and simple design would also work in a thinner-weight yarn for a smaller project.

YARN

Cascade 220® (aran/10-ply/worsted; 100g/3½oz; 200m/220yd)

	A	8505 White – 8 balls
	B	2433 Pacific – 1 ball
	C	1004 Bristol Blue – 1 ball
	D	1073 Water Spout – 1 ball
	E	1072 Key West – 1 ball
	F	9682 Desert Flower – 1 ball
	G	1070 Golden Kiwi – 2 balls

ABBREVIATIONS & STITCHES

ch   chain

ch sp chain space

dec   sl st in next 3 sts, sl st into 3-ch sp

inc   ch 6, 1 tr in fourth ch from hook, 1 tr in next 2 ch, sl st into ch sp of next block

RS   right side

sl st slip stitch

st(s) stitch(es)

tr   treble crochet

WS   wrong side

↙ / ↗ direction of work

Throw

↙ **Row 1 (RS):** using yarn A, ch 6, 1 tr in fourth ch from hook and in next 2 ch, turn (1 block).

↗ **Row 2 (WS):** inc, A x 1, turn (2 blocks).

↙ **Row 3 (RS):** inc, A x 2, turn (3 blocks).

↗ **Row 4 (WS):** inc, A x 3, turn (4 blocks).

↙ **Row 5 (RS):** inc, A x 4, turn (5 blocks).

↗ **Row 6 (WS):** inc, A x 5, turn (6 blocks).

↙ **Row 7 (RS):** inc, A x 6, changing to yarn B when working last st, fasten off yarn A, turn (7 blocks).

↗ **Row 8 (WS):** inc, B x 7, turn (8 blocks).

↙ **Row 9 (RS):** inc, B x 8, turn (9 blocks).

↗ **Row 10 (WS):** inc, B x 9, turn (10 blocks).

↙ **Row 11 (RS):** inc, B x 10, turn (11 blocks).

↗ **Row 12 (WS):** inc, B x 11, changing to yarn A when working last st, fasten off yarn B, turn (12 blocks).

↙ **Row 13 (RS):** inc, A x 12, turn (13 blocks).

↗ **Row 14 (WS):** inc, A x 13, turn (14 blocks).

↙ **Row 15 (RS):** inc, A x 14, turn (15 blocks).

↗ **Row 16 (WS):** inc, A x 15, changing to yarn C when working last st, fasten off yarn A, turn (16 blocks).

↙ **Row 17 (RS):** inc, C x 16, turn (17 blocks).

↗ **Row 18 (WS):** inc, C x 17, turn (18 blocks).

↙ **Row 19 (RS):** inc, C x 18, turn (19 blocks).

↗ **Row 20 (WS):** inc, C x 19, turn (20 blocks).

↙ **Row 21 (RS):** inc, C x 20, changing to yarn A when working last st, fasten off yarn C, turn (21 blocks).

↗ **Row 22 (WS):** inc, A x 21, turn (22 blocks).

↙ **Row 23 (RS):** inc, A x 22, turn (23 blocks).

↗ **Row 24 (WS):** inc, A x 23, turn (24 blocks).

↙ **Row 25 (RS):** inc, A x 24, changing to yarn D when working last st, fasten off yarn A, turn (25 blocks).

↗ **Row 26 (WS):** inc, D x 25, turn (26 blocks).

↙ **Row 27 (RS):** inc, D x 26, turn (27 blocks).

↗ **Row 28 (WS):** inc, D x 27, turn (28 blocks).

↙ **Row 29 (RS):** inc, D x 28, turn (29 blocks).

↗ **Row 30 (WS):** inc, D x 29, changing to yarn A when working last st, fasten off yarn D, turn (30 blocks).

↙ **Row 31 (RS):** inc, A x 30, turn (31 blocks).

↗ **Row 32 (WS):** inc, A x 31, turn (32 blocks).

↙ **Row 33 (RS):** inc, A x 32, turn (33 blocks).

↗ **Row 34 (WS):** inc, A x 33, changing to yarn E when working last st, fasten off yarn A, turn (34 blocks).

↙ Row 35 (RS): inc, E x 34, turn (35 blocks).

↗ Row 36 (WS): inc, E x 35, turn (36 blocks).

↙ Row 37 (RS): inc, E x 36, turn (37 blocks).

↗ Row 38 (WS): inc, E x 37, turn (38 blocks).

↙ Row 39 (RS): inc, E x 38, changing to yarn A when working last st, fasten off yarn E, turn (39 blocks).

↗ Row 40 (WS): inc, A x 39, turn (40 blocks).

↙ Row 41 (RS): inc, A x 40, turn (41 blocks).

↗ Row 42 (WS): inc, A x 41, turn (42 blocks).

↙ Row 43 (RS): inc, A x 42, changing to yarn F when working last st, fasten off yarn A, turn (43 blocks).

↗ Row 44 (WS): inc, F x 43, turn (44 blocks).

↙ Row 45 (RS): inc, F x 44, turn (45 blocks).

↗ Row 46 (WS): inc, F x 45, turn (46 blocks).

↙ Row 47 (RS): inc, F x 46, turn (47 blocks).

↙ Row 48 (WS): inc, F x 47, changing to yarn A when working last st, fasten off yarn F, turn (48 blocks).

↙ Row 49 (RS): inc, A x 48, turn (49 blocks).

↗ Row 50 (WS): inc, A x 49, turn (50 blocks).

↙ Row 51 (RS): inc, A x 50, turn (51 blocks).

↙ Row 52 (WS): inc, A x 51, changing to yarn G when working last st, fasten off yarn A, turn (52 blocks).

↙ Row 53 (RS): inc, G x 52, turn (53 blocks).

↗ Row 54 (WS): inc, G x 53, turn (54 blocks).

↙ Row 55 (RS): inc, G x 54, turn (55 blocks).

Corner: start decreasing on WS.

↗ Row 56 (WS): dec, G x 55, turn (55 blocks).

↙ Row 57 (RS): inc, G x 54, fasten off yarn G, turn (55 blocks).

↗ Row 58 (WS): join A in last ch sp made, A x 55, turn (55 blocks).

↙ Row 59 (RS): inc, A x 54, turn (55 blocks).

↗ Row 60 (WS): dec, A x 55, turn (55 blocks).

↙ Row 61 (RS): inc, A x 54, fasten off yarn A, turn (55 blocks).

↗ Row 62 (WS): join yarn B in last ch sp made, B x 3, A x 2, C x 3, A x 2, D x 3, A x 2, E x 3, A x 2, F x 3, A x 2, G x 3, A x 27, turn (55 blocks).

↙ Row 63 (RS): inc, A x 27, G x 2, A x 3, F x 2, A x 3, E x 2, A x 3, D x 2, A x 3, C x 2, A x 3, B x 2, turn (55 blocks).

↗ Row 64 (WS): dec, B x 2, A x 2, C x 3, A x 2, D x 3, A x 2, E x 3, A x 2, F x 3, A x 2, G x 3, A x 28, turn (55 blocks).

↙ Row 65 (RS): inc, A x 28, G x 2, A x 3, F x 2, A x 3, E x 2, A x 3, D x 2, A x 3, C x 2, A x 3, B x 1, turn (55 blocks).

↗ Row 66 (WS): dec, B x 1, fasten off yarn B, A x 2, C x 3, A x 2, D x 3, A x 2, E x 3, A x 2, F x 3, A x 2, G x 3, A x 29, turn (55 blocks).

↙ Row 67 (RS): inc, A x 29, G x 2, A x 3, F x 2, A x 3, E x 2, A x 3, D x 2, A x 3, C x 2, A x 3, turn (55 blocks).

↗ Row 68 (WS): dec, A x 2, C x 3, A x 2, D x 3, A x 2, E x 3, A x 2, F x 3, A x 2, G x 3, A x 30, turn (55 blocks).

↙ Row 69 (RS): inc, A x 30, G x 2, A x 3, F x 2, A x 3, E x 2, A x 3, D x 2, A x 3, C x 2, A x 2, turn (55 blocks).

↗ Row 70 (WS): dec, A x 1, C x 3, A x 2, D x 3, A x 2, E x 3, A x 2, F x 3, A x 2, G x 3, A x 31, turn (55 blocks).

↙ Row 71 (RS): inc, A x 31, G x 2, A x 3, F x 2, A x 3, E x 2, A x 3, D x 2, A x 3, C x 2, A x 1, fasten off yarn A, turn (55 blocks).

↗ Row 72 (WS): join yarn C in last ch sp made, C x 3, A x 2, D x 3, A x 2, E x 3, A x 2, F x 3, A x 2, G x 3, A x 32, turn (55 blocks).

↙ Row 73 (RS): inc, A x 32, G x 2, A x 3, F x 2, A x 3, E x 2, A x 3, D x 2, A x 3, C x 2, turn (55 blocks).

↗ Row 74 (WS): dec, C x 2, A x 2, D x 3, A x 2, E x 3, A x 2, F x 3, A x 2, G x 3, A x 33, turn (55 blocks).

↙ Row 75 (RS): inc, A x 33, G x 2, A x 3, F x 2, A x 3, E x 2, A x 3, D x 2, A x 3, C x 1, turn (55 blocks).

Corner: start decreasing on WS.

↗ Row 76 (WS): dec, C x 1, fasten off yarn C, A x 2, D x 3, A x 2, E x 3, A x 2, F x 3, A x 2, G x 3, A x 33, turn (54 blocks).

↙ Row 77 (RS): dec, A x 33, G x 2, A x 3, F x 2, A x 3, E x 2, A x 3, D x 2, A x 3, turn (53 blocks).

↗ Row 78 (WS): dec, A x 2, D x 3, A x 2, E x 3, A x 2, F x 3, A x 2, G x 3, A x 32, turn (52 blocks).

↙ Row 79 (RS): dec, A x 32, G x 2, A x 3, F x 2,
A x 3, E x 2, A x 3, D x 2, A x 2, turn (51 blocks).

↗ Row 80 (WS): dec, A x 1, D x 3, A x 2, E x 3, A x 2, F x 3, A x 2, G x 3, A x 31, turn (50 blocks).

↙ Row 81 (RS): dec, A x 31, G x 2, A x 3, F x 2, A x 3, E x 2, A x 3, D x 2, A x 1, fasten off yarn A, turn (49 blocks).

↗ Row 82 (WS): join yarn D in last ch sp made, D x 3, A x 2, E x 3, A x 2, F x 3, A x 2, G x 3, A x 30, turn (48 blocks).

↙ Row 83 (RS): dec, A x 30, G x 2, A x 3, F x 2, A x 3, E x 2, A x 3, D x 2, turn (47 blocks).

↗ Row 84 (WS): dec, D x 2, A x 2, E x 3, A x 2, F x 3, A x 2, G x 3, A x 29, turn (46 blocks).

↙ Row 85 (RS): dec, A x 29, G x 2, A x 3, F x 2, A x 3, E x 2, A x 3, D x 1, turn (45 blocks).

↗ Row 86 (WS): dec, D x 1, fasten off yarn D, A x 2, E x 3, A x 2, F x 3, A x 2, G x 3, A x 28, turn (44 blocks).

↙ Row 87 (RS): dec, A x 28, G x 2, A x 3, F x 2, A x 3, E x 2, A x 3, turn (43 blocks).

↗ Row 88 (WS): dec, A x 2, E x 3, A x 2, F x 3, A x 2, G x 3, A x 27, turn (42 blocks).

↙ Row 89 (RS): dec, A x 27, G x 2, A x 3, F x 2, A x 3, E x 2, A x 2, turn (41 blocks).

↗ Row 90 (WS): dec, A x 1, E x 3, A x 2, F x 3, A x 2, G x 3, A x 26, turn (40 blocks).

↙ Row 91 (RS): dec, A x 26, G x 2, A x 3, F x 2, A x 3, E x 2, A x 1, fasten off yarn A, turn (39 blocks).

↗ Row 92 (WS): join yarn E in last ch sp made, E x 3, A x 2, F x 3, A x 2, G x 3, A x 25, turn (38 blocks).

↙ Row 93 (RS): dec, A x 25, G x 2, A x 3, F x 2, A x 3, E x 2, turn (37 blocks).

↗ Row 94 (WS): dec, E x 2, A x 2, F x 3, A x 2, G x 3, A x 24, turn (36 blocks).

↙ Row 95 (RS): dec, A x 24, G x 2, A x 3, F x 2, A x 3, E x 1, turn (35 blocks).

↗ Row 96 (WS): dec, E x 1, fasten off yarn E, A x 2, F x 3, A x 2, G x 3, A x 23, turn (34 blocks).

↙ Row 97 (RS): dec, A x 23, G x 2, A x 3, F x 2, A x 3, turn (33 blocks).

↗ Row 98 (WS): dec, A x 2, F x 3, A x 2, G x 3, A x 22, turn (32 blocks).

↙ Row 99 (RS): dec, A x 22, G x 2, A x 3, F x 2, A x 2, turn (31 blocks).

↗ Row 100 (WS): dec, A x 1, F x 3, A x 2,
G x 3, A x 21, turn (30 blocks).

↙ Row 101 (RS): dec, A x 21, G x 2, A x 3, F x 2, A x 1, fasten off yarn A, turn (29 blocks).

↗ Row 102 (WS): dec, F x 3, A x 2, G x 3, A x 20, turn (28 blocks).

↙ Row 103 (RS): dec, A x 20, G x 2, A x 3, F x 2, turn (27 blocks).

↗ Row 104 (WS): dec, F x 2, A x 2, G x 3, A x 19, turn (26 blocks).

↙ Row 105 (RS): dec, A x 19, G x 2, A x 3, F x 1, turn (25 blocks).

↗ Row 106 (WS): dec, F x 1, fasten off yarn F, A x 2, G x 3, A x 18, turn (24 blocks).

↙ Row 107 (RS): dec, A x 18, G x 2, A x 3,turn (23 blocks).

↗ Row 108 (WS): dec, A x 2, G x 3, A x 17, turn (22 blocks).

↙ Row 109 (RS): dec, A x 17, G x 2, A x 2, turn (21 blocks).

↗ Row 110 (WS): dec, A x 1, G x 3, A x 16, turn (20 blocks).

↙ Row 111 (RS): dec, A x 16, G x 2, A x 1, turn (19 blocks).

↗ Row 112 (WS): dec, G x 3, A x 15, turn (18 blocks).

↙ Row 113 (RS): dec, A x 15, G x 2, turn (17 blocks).

↗ Row 114 (WS): dec, G x 2, A x 14, turn (16 blocks).

↙ Row 115 (RS): dec, A x 14, G x 1, turn (15 blocks).

↗ Row 116 (WS): dec, G x 1, fasten off yarn G, A x 13, turn (14 blocks).

↙ Row 117 (RS): dec, A x 13, turn (13 blocks).

↗ Row 118 (WS): dec, A x 12, turn (12 blocks).

↙ Row 119 (RS): dec, A x 11, turn (11 blocks).

↙ Row 120 (WS): dec, A x 10, turn (10 blocks).

↙ Row 121 (RS): dec, A x 9, turn (9 blocks).

↗ Row 122 (WS): dec, A x 8, turn (8 blocks).

↙ Row 123 (RS): dec, A x 7, turn (7 blocks).

↗ Row 124 (WS): dec, A x 6, turn (6 blocks).

↙ Row 125 (RS): dec, A x 5, turn (5 blocks).

↗ Row 126 (WS): dec, A x 4, turn (4 blocks).

↙ Row 127 (RS): dec, A x 3, turn (3 blocks).

↗ Row 128 (WS): dec, A x 2, turn (2 blocks).

↙ Row 129 (RS): dec, A x 1, fasten off yarn A (1 block).

Sew in all loose ends on WS of work.

Rhombus

This geometric design uses six colours in a chevron layout. Keep an eye on your yarn every few rows to avoid a tangle. You could try working this design with fewer colours, too.

SKILL LEVEL

☐ ☐ ☐

HOOK SIZE

6mm (US J-10)

BLOCK STITCH

3 tr block: (3 ch, 3 tr in ch sp)

THROW SIZE

122 x 163cm (48 x 64in)

YARN

Cascade 220® (aran/10-ply/worsted; 100g/3½oz; 200m/220yd)

🟥	A	9668 Paprika – 2 balls
🟧	B	1048 Camelia – 4 balls
🟧	C	9682 Desert Flower – 4 balls
🟩	D	1070 Golden Kiwi – 4 balls
🟩	E	1072 Key West – 14 balls
🟦	F	2433 Pacific – 2 balls

ABBREVIATIONS & STITCHES

ch	chain
ch sp	chain space
dec	sl st in next 3 sts, sl st into 3-ch sp
inc	ch 6, 1 tr in fourth ch from hook, 1 tr in next 2 ch, sl st into ch sp of next block
RS	right side
sl st	slip stitch
st(s)	stitch(es)
tr	treble crochet
WS	wrong side
↙ / ↗	direction of work

Throw

↙ **Row 1 (RS):** using yarn A, ch 6, 1 tr in fourth ch from hook, 1 tr in next 2 ch, turn (1 block).

↗ **Row 2 (WS):** inc, A x 1, turn (2 blocks).

↙ **Row 3 (RS):** inc, A x 2, turn (3 blocks).

↗ **Row 4 (WS):** inc, A x 3, turn (4 blocks).

↙ **Row 5 (RS):** inc, A x 4, turn (5 blocks).

↗ **Row 6 (WS):** inc, A x 5, turn (6 blocks).

↙ **Row 7 (RS):** inc, A x 6, turn (7 blocks).

↗ **Row 8 (WS):** inc, A x 7, changing to yarn B when working last st, fasten off yarn A, turn (8 blocks).

↙ **Row 9 (RS):** inc, B x 8, changing to yarn A when working last st, turn (9 blocks).

↗ **Row 10 (WS):** inc in A, B x 9, turn (10 blocks).

↙ **Row 11 (RS):** inc, B x 8, A x 2, turn (11 blocks).

↗ **Row 12 (WS):** inc, A x 2, B x 9, turn (12 blocks).

↙ **Row 13 (RS):** inc, B x 8, A x 4, turn (13 blocks).

↗ **Row 14 (WS):** inc, A x 4, B x 9, turn (14 blocks).

↙ **Row 15 (RS):** inc, B x 8, A x 6, turn (15 blocks).

↗ **Row 16 (WS):** inc, A x 6, B x 9, changing to yarn C when working last st, fasten off yarn B, turn (16 blocks).

↙ **Row 17 (RS):** inc, C x 8, A x 8, changing to yarn B when working last st, fasten off yarn A, turn (17 blocks).

↗ **Row 18 (WS):** inc, B x 8, C x 9, turn (18 blocks).

↙ **Row 19 (RS):** inc, C x 8, B x 9, A x 1, turn (19 blocks).

↗ **Row 20 (WS):** inc, A x 1, B x 9, C x 9, turn (20 blocks).

↙ **Row 21 (RS):** inc, C x 8, B x 9, A x 3, turn (21 blocks).

↗ **Row 22 (WS):** inc, A x 3, B x 9, C x 9, turn (22 blocks).

↙ **Row 23 (RS):** inc, C x 8, B x 9, A x 5, turn (23 blocks).

↗ **Row 24 (WS):** inc, A x 5, B x 9, C x 9, changing to yarn D when working last st, fasten off yarn C, turn (24 blocks).

↙ **Row 25 (RS):** inc, D x 8, B x 9, A x 7, turn (25 blocks).

↗ **Row 26 (WS):** inc, A x 7, C x 9, D x 9, turn (26 blocks).

↙ **Row 27 (RS):** inc, D x 8, C x 9, B x 9, changing to yarn A when working last st, turn (27 blocks).

↗ **Row 28 (WS):** inc in A, B x 9, C x 9, D x 9, turn (28 blocks).

↙ **Row 29 (RS):** inc, D x 8, C x 9, B x 9, A x 2, turn (29 blocks).

↗ **Row 30 (WS):** inc, A x 2, B x 9, C x 9, D x 9, turn (30 blocks).

↙ **Row 31 (RS):** inc, D x 8, C x 9, B x 9, A x 4, turn (31 blocks).

↗ **Row 32 (WS):** inc, A x 4, B x 9, C x 9, D x 9, changing to yarn E when working last st, fasten off yarn D, turn (32 blocks).

↙ **Row 33 (RS):** inc, E x 8, C x 9, fasten off yarn C, B x 9, A x 6, turn (33 blocks).

↗ **Row 34 (WS):** inc, A x 6, B x 9, fasten off yarn B, D x 9, E x 9, turn (34 blocks).

↙ **Row 35 (RS):** inc, E x 8, D x 9, C x 9, A x 8, changing to yarn B when working last st,

fasten off yarn A, turn (35 blocks).

↗ **Row 36 (WS):** inc, B x 8, C x 9, D x 9, E x 9, turn (36 blocks).

↙ **Row 37 (RS):** inc, E x 8, D x 9, C x 9, B x 9, A x 1, turn (37 blocks).

↗ **Row 38 (WS):** inc in A, B x 10, C x 9, D x 9, E x 9, turn (38 blocks).

↙ **Row 39 (RS):** inc, E x 8, D x 9, C x 9, B x 10, A x 2, turn (39 blocks).

↗ **Row 40 (WS):** inc, A x 1, B x 11, C x 9, D x 9, E x 9 changing to yarn F when working last st, fasten off yarn E, turn (40 blocks).

↙ **Row 41 (RS):** inc, F x 8, D x 9, fasten off yarn D, C x 9, B x 11, A x 3, turn (41 blocks).

↗ **Row 42 (WS):** inc, A x 2, B x 12, C x 9, fasten off yarn C, E x 9, F x 9, turn (42 blocks).

↙ **Row 43 (RS):** inc, F x 8, E x 9, D x 9, B x 12, A x 4, turn (43 blocks).

↗ **Row 44 (WS):** inc, A x 3, B x 4, C x 9, D x 9, E x 9, F x 9, turn (44 blocks).

↙ **Row 45 (RS):** inc, F x 8, E x 9, D x 9, C x 9, B x 4, A x 4, B x 1 changing to yarn A when working last st, turn (45 blocks).

↗ **Row 46 (WS):** inc in A, B x 1, A x 3, B x 4, C x 10, D x 9, E x 9, F x 9, turn (46 blocks).

↙ **Row 47 (RS):** inc, F x 8, E x 9, D x 9, C x 10, B x 4, A x 3, B x 2, A x 1, turn (47 blocks).

↗ **Row 48 (WS):** inc, A x 1, B x 2, A x 2, B x 4, C x 11, D x 9, E x 9, F x 9, turn (48 blocks).

↙ **Row 49 (RS):** inc, F x 8, fasten off yarn F, E x 9, fasten off yarn E, D x 9, C x 11, B x 4, A x 2, B x 3, A x 2, turn (49 blocks).

↗ **Row 50 (WS):** inc, A x 2, B x 3, A x 1, B x 4, C x 12, D x 9, fasten off yarn D, F x 9, E x 9, turn (50 blocks).

↙ **Row 51 (RS):** inc, E x 9, F x 9, E x 9, C x 12, B x 4, fasten off yarn B, A x 1, B x 4, A x 3, turn (51 blocks).

↙ **Row 52 (WS):** inc, A x 3, B x 8, C x 4, D x 9, E x 9, F x 9, E x 9, turn (52 blocks).

↙ **Row 53 (RS):** inc, E x 8, F x 9, E x 9, D x 9, C x 4, B x 4, C x 1, B x 4, A x 4 changing to yarn B when working last st, turn (53 blocks).

↙ **Row 54 (WS):** inc in B, A x 4, B x 4, C x 1, B x 3, C x 4, D x 10, E x 9, F x 9, E x 9, turn (54 blocks).

↙ **Row 55 (RS):** inc, E x 8, F x 9, E x 9, D x 10, C x 4, B x 3, C x 2, B x 4, A x 3, B x 1, A x 1, turn (55 blocks).

↗ **Row 56 (WS):** inc in A, B x 2, A x 3, B x 4, C x 2, B x 2, C x 4, D x 11, E x 9, F x 9, E x 9, turn (56 blocks).

↙ **Row 57 (RS):** inc, E x 8, fasten off yarn E, F x 9, E x 9, D x 11, C x 4, B x 2, C x 3, B x 4, A x 2, B x 2, A x 2, turn (57 blocks).

↗ **Row 58 (WS):** inc, A x 1, B x 3, A x 2, B x 4, C x 3, B, C x 4, D x 12, E x 9, fasten off yarn E, F x 9, fasten off yarn F, D x 9, turn (58 blocks).

↙ **Row 59 (RS):** inc, D x 8, E x 9, F x 9, D x 12, C x 4, fasten off yarn C, B x 1, fasten off yarn B, C x 4, B x 4, A x 1, B x 3, A x 3, turn (59 blocks).

↗ **Row 60 (WS):** inc, A x 2, B x 4, fasten off yarn B, A x 1, fasten off yarn A, B x 4, C x 8, D x 4, E x 9, F x 9, E x 9, D x 9, turn (60 blocks).

↙ **Row 61 (RS):** inc, D x 8, E x 9, F x 9, E x 9, D x 4, C x 4, D, C x 4, B x 8, A x 4, turn (61 blocks).

↗ **Row 62 (WS):** inc, A x 3, B x 4, C x 1, B x 4, C x 4, D, C x 3, D x 4, E x 10, F x 9, E x 9, D x 9, turn (62 blocks).

Corner: start decreasing on WS.

↙ **Row 63 (RS):** inc, D x 8, E x 9, F x 9, E x 10, D x 4, C x 3, D x 2, C x 4, B x 3, C x 1, B x 4, A x 4, turn (62 blocks).

↗ **Row 64 (WS):** dec, A x 3, B x 4, C x 2, B x 3, C x 4, D x 2, C x 2, D x 4, E x 11, F x 9, E x 9, D x 9, turn (62 blocks).

↙ **Row 65 (RS):** inc, D x 8, fasten off yarn D,

E x 9, F x 9, E x 11, D x 4, C x 2, D x 3, C x 4, B x 2, C x 2, B x 4, A x 3, turn (62 blocks).

↗ **Row 66 (WS):** dec, A x 2, B x 4, C x 3, B x 2, C x 4, D x 3, C x 1, D x 4, E x 12, F x 9, E x 9, C x 9, turn (62 blocks).

↙ **Row 67 (RS):** inc, C x 8, D x 9, F x 9, fasten off yarn F, E x 12, D x 4, C x 1, fasten off yarn C, D x 4, fasten off yarn D, C x 4, B x 2, C x 3, B x 4, A x 2, turn (62 blocks).

↗ **Row 68 (WS):** dec, A x 1, B x 4, C x 4, fasten off yarn C, B x 1, fasten off yarn B, C x 4, D x 8, E x 4, F x 9, E x 9, D x 9, C x 9, turn (62 blocks).

↙ **Row 69 (RS):** inc, C x 9, D x 9, E x 9, F x 9, E x 4, D x 4, E x 1, D x 4, C x 8, B x 4, A x 1, fasten off yarn A, turn (62 blocks).

↗ **Row 70 (WS):** pick up B in last ch sp made, dec, B x 4, C x 4, D x 1, C x 4, D x 4, E x 1, D x 3, E x 4, F x 10, E x 9, D x 9, C x 9, turn (62 blocks).

↙ **Row 71 (RS):** inc, C x 8, D x 9, E x 9, F x 10, E x 4, D x 3, E x 2, D x 4, C x 3, D, C x 4, B x 4, turn (62 blocks).

↗ **Row 72 (WS):** dec, B x 3, C x 4, D x 2, C x 3, D x 4, E x 2, D x 2, E x 4, F x 11, E x 9, D x 9, C x 9, turn (62 blocks).

↙ **Row 73 (RS):** inc, C x 8, fasten off yarn C, D x 9, E x 9, F x 11, E x 4, D x 2, E x 3, D x 4, C x 2, D x 2, C x 4, B x 3, turn (62 blocks).

↗ **Row 74 (WS):** dec, B x 2, C x 4, D x 3, C x 2, D x 4, E x 3, D x 1, E x 4, F x 12, E x 9, D x 9, fasten off yarn D, B x 9, turn (62 blocks).

↙ **Row 75 (RS):** inc, B x 8, C x 9, E x 9, fasten off yarn E, F x 12, E x 4, fasten off yarn E, D x 1, fasten off yarn D, E x 4, D x 4, C x 1, D x 3, C x 4, B x 2, turn (62 blocks).

↗ **Row 76 (WS):** dec, B x 1, C x 4, D x 4, fasten off yarn D, C x 1, fasten off yarn C, D x 4, E x 8, F x 13, fasten off yarn F, D x 9, C x 9, B x 9, turn (62 blocks).

↙ **Row 77 (RS):** inc, B x 8, C x 9, D x 9, E x 9, F x 4, E x 4, F x 1, E x 4, D x 8, C x 4, B x 1, fasten off yarn B, turn (62 blocks).

↗ **Row 78 (WS):** pick up yarn C in last ch sp made, dec, C x 4, D x 4, E, D x 4, E x 4, F x 1, E x 3, F x 5, E x 9, D x 9, C x 9, B x 9, turn (62 blocks).

↙ **Row 79 (RS):** inc, B x 8, C x 9, D x 9, E x 10, F x 4, E x 3, F x 2, E x 4, D x 3, E, D x 4, C x 4, turn (62 blocks).

↗ **Row 80 (WS):** dec, C x 3, D x 4, E x 2, D x 3, E x 4, F x 2, E x 2, F x 5, E x 10, D x 9, C x 9, B x 9, turn (62 blocks).

↙ **Row 81 (RS):** inc, B x 8, fasten off yarn B, C x 9, D x 9, E x 11, F x 4, E x 2, F x 3, E x 4, D x 2, E x 2, D x 4, C x 3, turn (62 blocks).

Corner: start decreasing on RS.

↗ **Row 82 (WS):** dec, C x 2, D x 4, E x 3, D x 2, E x 4, F x 3, E x 1, F x 5, E x 11, D x 9, C x 9, fasten off yarn C, A x 8, turn (61 blocks).

↙ **Row 83 (RS):** dec, A x 8, B x 9, D x 9, fasten off yarn D, E x 12, F x 4, E x 1, fasten off yarn E, F x 4, E x 4, D x 1, E x 3, D x 4, C x 2, turn (60 blocks).

↗ **Row 84 (WS):** dec, C x 1, D x 4, E x 4, D x 1, fasten off yarn D, E x 4, F x 9, E x 12, fasten off yarn E, C x 9, B x 9, A x 6, turn (59 blocks).

↙ **Row 85 (RS):** dec, A x 5, B x 9, C x 9, D x 9, E x 4, F x 9, E x 8, D x 4, C x 1, fasten off yarn C, turn (58 blocks).

↗ **Row 86 (WS):** pick up yarn D in last ch sp made, dec, D x 4, E x 4, F x 1, E x 4, F x 4, E x 1, F x 4, E x 4, D x 9, C x 9, B x 9, A x 4, turn (57 blocks).

↙ **Row 87 (RS):** dec, A x 3, B x 9, C x 9, D x 10, E x 4, F x 3, E x 1, F x 5, E x 3, F x 1, E x 4, D x 4, turn (56 blocks).

↗ **Row 88 (WS):** dec, D x 3, E x 4, F x 2, E x 3,

F x 4, E x 2, F x 3, E x 4, D x 10, C x 9, B x 9, A x 2, turn (55 blocks).

↙ Row 89 (RS): dec, A x 1, fasten off yarn A, B x 9, C x 9, D x 11, E x 4, F x 2, E x 2, F x 5, E x 2, F x 2, E x 4, D x 3, turn (54 blocks).

↗ Row 90 (WS): dec, D x 2, E x 4, F x 3, E x 2, F x 4, E x 3, F x 2, E x 4, D x 11, C x 9, B x 9, fasten off yarn B, turn (53 blocks).

↙ Row 91 (RS): pick up yarn A in last ch sp made, dec, A x 8, C x 9, fasten off yarn C, D x 12, E x 4, F x 1, E x 3, F x 5, E x 1, F x 3, E x 4, D x 2, turn (52 blocks).

↗ Row 92 (WS): dec, D x 1, E x 4, F x 4, E x 1, fasten off yarn E, F x 4, E x 4, fasten off yarn E, F x 1, fasten off yarn F, E x 4, D x 12, fasten off yarn D, B x 9, A x 7, turn (51 blocks).

↙ Row 93 (RS): dec, A x 6, B x 9, C x 9, D x 4, E x 8, F x 9, E x 4, D x 1, fasten off yarn D, turn (50 blocks).

↗ Row 94 (WS): pick up yarn E in last ch sp made, dec, E x 4, F x 9, E x 4, D x 1, E x 4, D x 4, C x 9, B x 9, A x 5, turn (49 blocks).

↙ Row 95 (RS): dec, A x 4, B x 9, C x 10, D x 4, E x 3, D x 1, E x 4, F x 4, E x 1, F x 4, E x 4, turn (48 blocks).

↗ Row 96 (WS): dec, E x 3, F x 5, E x 1, F x 3, E x 4, D x 2, E x 3, D x 4, C x 10, B x 9, A x 3, turn (47 blocks).

↙ Row 97 (RS): dec, A x 2, B x 9, C x 11, D x 4, E x 2, D x 2, E x 4, F x 3, E x 2, F x 4, E x 3, turn (46 blocks).

↗ Row 98 (WS): dec, E x 2, F x 5, E x 2, F x 2, E x 4, D x 3, E x 2, D x 4, C x 11, B x 9, A x 1, fasten off yarn A, turn (45 blocks).

↙ Row 99 (RS): pick up yarn B in last ch sp made, dec, B x 9, fasten off yarn B, C x 12, D x 4, E x 1, D x 3, E x 4, F x 2, E x 3, F x 4, E x 2, turn (44 blocks).

↗ Row 100 (WS): dec, E x 1, F x 5, E x 3, F x 1, E x 4, D x 4, E x 1, fasten off yarn E, D x 4, C x 12, fasten off yarn C, A x 8, turn (43 blocks).

↙ Row 101 (RS): dec, A x 7, B x 9, C x 4, D x 8, E x 4, fasten off yarn E, F x 1, fasten off yarn F, E x 4, F x 4, E x 1, fasten off yarn E, turn (42 blocks).

↗ Row 102 (WS): pick up yarn F in last ch sp made, dec, F x 5, E x 8, D x 4, C x 1, D x 4, C x 4, B x 9, A x 6, turn (41 blocks).

↙ Row 103 (RS): dec, A x 5, B x 10, C x 4,

D x 3, C, D x 4, E x 4, D x 1, E x 4, F x 4, turn (40 blocks).

↗ Row 104 (WS): dec, F x 4, E x 4, D x 1, E x 3, D x 4, C x 2, D x 3, C x 4, B x 10, A x 4, turn (39 blocks).

↙ Row 105 (RS): dec, A x 3, B x 11, C x 4, D x 2, C x 2, D x 4, E x 3, D x 2, E x 4, F x 3, turn (38 blocks).

↗ Row 106 (WS): dec, F x 3, E x 4, D x 2, E x 2, D x 4, C x 3, D x 2, C x 4, B x 11, A x 2, turn (37 blocks).

↙ Row 107 (RS): dec, A x 1, fasten off yarn A, B x 12, C x 4, D, C x 3, D x 4, E x 2, D x 3, E x 4, F x 2, turn (36 blocks).

↗ Row 108 (WS): dec, F x 2, E x 4, D x 3, E x 1, D x 4, fasten off yarn D, C x 4, D x 1, C x 4, B x 12, fasten off yarn B, turn (35 blocks).

↙ Row 109 (RS): pick up yarn A in last ch sp made, dec, A x 8, B x 4, C x 8, D x 4, fasten off yarn D, E x 1, fasten off yarn E, D x 4, E x 4, F x 1, turn (34 blocks).

↗ Row 110 (WS): dec, F x 1, E x 4, D x 8, C x 4, B x 1, C x 4, B x 4, A x 7, turn (33 blocks).

↙ Row 111 (RS): dec, A x 7, B x 4, C x 3, B, C x 4, D x 4, C x 1, D x 4, E x 4, turn (32 blocks).

↗ Row 112 (WS): dec, E x 4, D x 4, C x 1, D x 3, C x 4, B x 2, C x 3, B x 4, A x 6, turn (31 blocks).

↙ Row 113 (RS): dec, A x 6, B x 4, C x 2, B x 2, C x 4, D x 3, C x 2, D x 4, E x 3, turn (30 blocks).

↗ Row 114 (WS): dec, E x 3, D x 4, C x 2, D x 2, C x 4, B x 3, C x 2, B x 4, A x 5, turn (29 blocks).

↙ Row 115 (RS): dec, A x 5, B x 4, C x 1, B x 3, C x 4, D x 2, C x 3, D x 4, E x 2, turn (28 blocks).

↗ Row 116 (WS): dec, E x 2, D x 4, C x 3, D x 1, C x 4, B x 4, fasten off yarn B, C x 1, fasten off yarn C, B x 4, A x 4, turn (27 blocks).

↙ Row 117 (RS): dec, A x 4, B x 8, C x 4, D x 1, C x 4, D x 4, E x 1, turn (26 blocks).

↗ Row 118 (WS): dec, E x 1, fasten off yarn E, D x 4, C x 8, B x 4, A x 1, B x 4, A x 3, turn (25 blocks).

↙ Row 119 (RS): dec, A x 3, B x 3, A, B x 4, C x 4, B x 1, C x 4, D x 4, turn (24 blocks).

↗ Row 120 (WS): dec, D x 4, C x 4, B x 1, C x 3, B x 4, A x 2, B x 3, A x 2, turn (23 blocks).

↙ Row 121 (RS): dec, A x 2, B x 2, A x 2, B x 4, C x 3, B x 2, C x 4, D x 3, turn (22 blocks).

↗ Row 122 (WS): dec, D x 3, C x 4, B x 2, C x 2, B x 4, A x 3, B x 2, A x 1, turn (21 blocks).

↙ Row 123 (RS): dec, A x 1, fasten off yarn A, B, A x 3, B x 4, C x 2, B x 3, C x 4, D x 2, turn (20 blocks).

↗ Row 124 (WS): dec, D x 2, C x 4, B x 3, C x 1, B x 4, A x 4, B x 1, fasten off yarn B, turn (19 blocks).

↙ Row 125 (RS): pick up yarn A in last ch sp made, dec, A x 4, B x 4, C x 1, fasten off yarn C, B x 4, C x 4, D x 1, turn (18 blocks).

↗ Row 126 (WS): dec, D x 1, C x 4, B x 8, A x 4, turn (17 blocks).

↙ Row 127 (RS): dec, A x 3, B x 4, A x 1, B x 4, C x 4, turn (16 blocks).

↗ Row 128 (WS): dec, C x 4, B x 4, A x 1, B x 3, A x 3, turn (15 blocks).

↙ Row 129 (RS): dec, A x 2, B x 3, A x 2, B x 4, C x 3, turn (14 blocks).

↗ Row 130 (WS): dec, C x 3, B x 4, A x 2, B x 2, A x 2, turn (13 blocks).

↙ Row 131 (RS): dec, A x 1, B x 2, A x 3, B x 4, C x 2, turn (12 blocks).

↗ Row 132 (WS): dec, C x 2, B x 4, A x 3, B x 2, A x 1, fasten off yarn A, turn (11 blocks).

↙ Row 133 (RS): pick up yarn B in last ch sp made, dec, B x 1, A x 4, B x 4, C x 1, turn (10 blocks).

↗ Row 134 (WS): dec, C x 1, fasten off yarn C, B x 4, A x 4, turn (9 blocks).

↙ Row 135 (RS): dec, A x 4, B x 4, turn (8 blocks).

↗ Row 136 (WS): dec, B x 4, A x 3, turn (7 blocks).

↙ Row 137 (RS): dec, A x 3, B x 3, turn (6 blocks).

↗ Row 138 (WS): dec, B x 3, A x 2, turn (5 blocks).

↙ Row 139 (RS): dec, A x 2, B x 2, turn (4 blocks).

↗ Row 140 (WS): dec, B x 2, A x 1, turn (3 blocks).

↙ Row 141 (RS): dec, A x 1, fasten off yarn A, B x 1, turn (2 blocks).

↗ Row 142 (WS): dec, B x 1, fasten off yarn B (1 block).

Sew in all loose ends on WS of work.

Zigzags

This is a simpler zigzag design that can be worked in any colourway you like. Increase or reduce the number of colours as you wish!

SKILL LEVEL

HOOK SIZE

6mm (US J-10)

BLOCK STITCH

3 tr block: (3 ch, 3 tr in ch sp)

THROW SIZE

98 x 132cm (38½ x 52in)

YARN

Cascade 220® (aran/10-ply/worsted; 100g/3½oz; 200m/220yd)

- **A** 8509 Grey – 3 balls
- **B** 1054 Mallard Blue – 2 balls
- **C** 9634 Aqua Haze – 2 balls
- **D** 1069 Anise Flower – 2 balls
- **E** 1049 Peach Dust – 2 balls

ABBREVIATIONS & STITCHES

ch	chain
ch sp	chain space
dec	sl st in next 3 sts, sl st into 3-ch sp
inc	ch 6, 1 tr in fourth ch from hook, 1 tr in next 2 ch, sl st into ch sp of next block
RS	right side
sl st	slip stitch
st(s)	stitch(es)
tr	treble crochet
WS	wrong side
↙/↗	direction of work

Throw

↙ **Row 1 (RS):** using yarn A, ch 6, 1 tr in fourth ch from hook, 1 tr in next 2 ch, turn (1 block).

↗ **Row 2 (WS):** inc, A x 1, turn (2 blocks).

↙ **Row 3 (RS):** inc, A x 2, turn (3 blocks).

↗ **Row 4 (WS):** inc, A x 3 changing to yarn B when working last st, fasten off yarn A, turn (4 blocks).

↙ **Row 5 (RS):** inc, B x 4 changing to yarn A when working last st, turn (5 blocks).

↗ **Row 6 (WS):** inc in A, B x 5, turn (6 blocks).

↙ **Row 7 (RS):** inc, B x 5, A x 1, turn (7 blocks).

↗ **Row 8 (WS):** inc, A x 1, B x 6 changing to yarn C when working last st, turn (8 blocks).

↙ **Row 9 (RS):** inc, C x 4, B x 2, A x 2, turn (9 blocks).

↗ **Row 10 (WS):** inc, A x 2, B x 2, C x 5, turn (10 blocks).

↙ **Row 11 (RS):** inc, C x 5, B x 2, A x 3, turn (11 blocks).

↗ **Row 12 (WS):** inc, A x 3, B x 2, C x 6 changing to yarn D when working last st, turn (12 blocks).

↙ **Row 13 (RS):** inc, D x 4, C x 2, B x 6 changing to yarn A when working last st, turn (13 blocks).

↗ **Row 14 (WS):** inc in A, B x 6, C x 2, D x 5, turn (14 blocks).

↙ **Row 15 (RS):** inc, D x 5, C x 2, B x 6, A x 1, turn (15 blocks).

↗ **Row 16 (WS):** inc, A x 1, B x 6, C x 2, D x 6 changing to yarn E when working last st, turn (16 blocks).

↙ **Row 17 (RS):** inc, E x 4, D x 2, C x 6, B x 2, A x 2, turn (17 blocks).

↗ **Row 18 (WS):** inc, A x 2, B x 2, C x 6, D x 2, E x 5, turn (18 blocks).

↙ **Row 19 (RS):** inc, E x 5, D x 2, C x 6, B x 2, A x 3, turn (19 blocks).

↗ **Row 20 (WS):** inc, A x 3, B x 2, C x 6, D x 2, E x 6, turn (20 blocks).

↙ **Row 21 (RS):** inc, A x 4, E x 2, D x 6, C x 2, B x 6 changing to yarn A when working last st, turn (21 blocks).

↗ **Row 22 (WS):** inc in A, B x 6, C x 2, D x 6, E x 2, A x 5, turn (22 blocks).

↙ **Row 23 (RS):** inc, A x 5, E x 2, D x 6, C x 2, B x 6, A x 1, turn (23 blocks).

↗ **Row 24 (WS):** inc, A x 1, B x 6, C x 2, D x 6, E x 2, A x 6 changing to yarn B when working last st, turn (24 blocks).

↙ **Row 25 (RS):** inc, B x 4, A x 2, E x 6, D x 2, C x 6, B x 2, A x 2, turn (25 blocks).

↗ **Row 26 (WS):** inc, A x 2, B x 2, C x 6, D x 2, E x 6, A x 2, B x 5, turn (26 blocks).

↙ **Row 27 (RS):** inc, B x 5, A x 2, E x 6, D x 2, C x 6, B x 2, A x 3, turn (27 blocks).

↗ **Row 28 (WS):** inc, A x 3, B x 2, C x 6, D x 2, E x 6, A x 2, B x 6 changing to yarn C when working last st, turn (28 blocks).

↙ **Row 29 (RS):** inc, C x 4, B x 2, A x 6, E x 2, D x 6, C x 2, B x 6 changing to yarn A when working last st, turn (29 blocks).

↗ **Row 30 (WS):** inc in A, B x 6, C x 2, D x 6, E x 2, A x 6, B x 2, C x 5, turn (30 blocks).

↙ **Row 31 (RS):** inc, C x 5, B x 2, A x 6, E x 2, D x 6, C x 2, B x 6, A x 1, turn (31 blocks).

↗ **Row 32 (WS):** inc, A x 1, B x 6, C x 2, D x 6, E x 2, A x 6, B x 2, C x 6, changing to yarn D when working last st, turn (32 blocks).

↙ **Row 33 (RS):** inc, D x 4, C x 2, B x 6, A x 2, E x 6, D x 2, C x 6, B x 2, A x 2, turn (33 blocks).

↗ **Row 34 (WS):** inc, A x 2, B x 2, C x 6, D x 2, E x 6, A x 2, B x 6, C x 2, D x 5, turn (34 blocks).

↙ **Row 35 (RS):** inc, D x 5, C x 2, B x 6, A x 2, E x 6, D x 2, C x 6, B x 2, A x 3, turn (35 blocks).

↗ **Row 36 (WS):** inc, A x 3, B x 2, C x 6, D x 2, E x 6, A x 2, B x 6, C x 2, D x 6 changing to yarn E when working last st, turn (36 blocks).

↙ **Row 37 (RS):** inc, E x 4, D x 2, C x 6, B x 2, A x 6, E x 2, D x 6, C x 2, B x 6 changing to yarn A when working last st, turn (37 blocks).

↗ **Row 38 (WS):** inc in A, B x 6, C x 2, D x 6, E x 2, A x 6, B x 2, C x 6, D x 2, E x 5, turn (38 blocks).

↙ **Row 39 (RS):** inc, E x 5, D x 2, C x 6, B x 2, A x 6, E x 2, D x 6, C x 2, B x 6, A x 1, turn (39 blocks).

↗ **Row 40 (WS):** inc, A x 1, B x 6, C x 2, D x 6, E x 2, A x 6, B x 2, C x 6, D x 2, E x 6 changing to yarn A when working last st, turn (40 blocks).

↙ **Row 41 (RS):** inc, A x 4, E x 2, D x 6, C x 2, B x 6, A x 2, E x 6, D x 2, C x 6, B x 2, A x 2, turn (41 blocks).

↗ **Row 42 (WS):** inc, A x 2, B x 2, C x 6, D x 2, E x 6, A x 2, B x 6, C x 2, D x 6, E x 2, A x 5, turn (42 blocks).

↙ **Row 43 (RS):** inc, A x 5, E x 2, D x 6, C x 2, B x 6, A x 2, E x 6, D x 2, C x 6, B x 2, A x 3, turn (43 blocks).

↗ **Row 44 (WS):** inc, A x 3, B x 2, C x 6, D x 2, E x 6, A x 2, B x 6, C x 2, D x 6, E x 2, A x 6, turn (44 blocks).

↙ **Row 45 (RS):** inc, A x 6, E x 6, D x 2, C x 6, B x 2, A x 6, E x 2, D x 6, C x 2, B x 6 changing to yarn A when working last st, turn (45 blocks).

↗ **Row 46 (WS):** inc in A, B x 6, C x 2, D x 6, E x 2, A x 6, B x 2, C x 6, D x 2, E x 6, A x 2, B x 5, turn (46 blocks).

↙ **Row 47 (RS):** inc, B x 4, A x 3, E x 6, D x 2, C x 6, B x 2, A x 6, E x 2, D x 6, C x 2, B x 6, A x 1, turn (47 blocks).

↗ **Row 48 (WS):** inc, A x 1, B x 6, C x 2, D x 6, E x 2, A x 6, B x 2, C x 6, D x 2, E x 6, A x 2, B x 6, turn (48 blocks).

↙ **Row 49 (RS):** inc, B x 5, A x 7, E x 2, D x 6, C x 2, B x 6, A x 2, E x 6, D x 2, C x 6, B x 2, A x 2, turn (49 blocks).

Corner: start decreasing on WS.

↗ **Row 50 (WS):** dec, A x 2, B x 2, C x 6, D x 2, E x 6, A x 2, B x 6, C x 2, D x 6, E x 2, A x 6, B x 2, C x 5, turn (49 blocks).

↙ **Row 51 (RS):** inc, C x 4, B x 2, A x 7, E x 2, D x 6, C x 2, B x 6, A x 2, E x 6, D x 2, C x 6, B x 2, A x 1, turn (49 blocks).

↗ **Row 52 (WS):** dec, A x 1, B x 2, C x 6, D x 2, E x 6, A x 2, B x 6, C x 2, D x 6, E x 2, A x 6, B x 2, C x 6, turn (49 blocks).

↙ **Row 53 (RS):** inc, C x 5, B x 2, A x 7, E x 6, D x 2, C x 6, B x 2, A x 6, E x 2, D x 6, C x 2, B x 2, turn (49 blocks).

↗ **Row 54 (WS):** dec, B x 2, C x 2, D x 6, E x 2, A x 6, B x 2, C x 6, D x 2, E x 6, A x 2, B x 6, C x 2, D x 5, turn (49 blocks).

↙ **Row 55 (RS):** inc, D x 4, C x 2, B x 6, A x 3, E x 6, D x 2, C x 6, B x 2, A x 6, E x 2, D x 6, C x 2, B x 1, turn (49 blocks).

↗ **Row 56 (WS):** dec, B x 1, C x 2, D x 6, E x 2, A x 6, B x 2, C x 6, D x 2, E x 6, A x 2, B x 6, C x 2, D x 6, turn (49 blocks).

↙ **Row 57 (RS):** inc, D x 5, C x 2, B x 6, A x 7, E x 2, D x 6, C x 2, B x 6, A x 2, E x 6, D x 2, C x 2, turn (49 blocks).

↗ **Row 58 (WS):** dec, C x 2, D x 2, E x 6, A x 2, B x 6, C x 2, D x 6, E x 2, A x 6, B x 2, C x 6, D x 2, E x 5, turn (49 blocks).

↙ **Row 59 (RS):** inc, E x 4, D x 2, C x 6, B x 2, A x 7, E x 2, D x 6, C x 2, B x 6, A x 2, E x 6, D x 2, C x 1, turn (49 blocks).

↗ **Row 60 (WS):** dec, C x 1, D x 2, E x 6, A x 2, B x 6, C x 2, D x 6, E x 2, A x 6, B x 2, C x 6, D x 2, E x 6, turn (49 blocks).

↙ **Row 61 (RS):** inc, E x 5, D x 2, C x 6, B x 2, A x 7, E x 6, D x 2, C x 6, B x 2, A x 6, E x 2, D x 2, turn (49 blocks).

↗ **Row 62 (WS):** dec, D x 2, E x 2, A x 6, B x 2, C x 6, D x 2, E x 6, A x 2, B x 6, C x 2, D x 6, E x 7, turn (49 blocks).

↙ **Row 63 (RS):** inc, A x 4, E x 2, D x 6, C x 2, B x 6, A x 3, E x 6, D x 2, C x 6, B x 2, A x 6, E x 2, D x 1, turn (49 blocks).

↗ **Row 64 (WS):** dec, D x 1, E x 2, A x 6, B x 2, C x 6, D x 2, E x 6, A x 2, B x 6, C x 2, D x 6, E x 3, A x 5, turn (49 blocks).

↙ **Row 65 (RS):** inc, A x 6, E x 2, D x 6, C x 2, B x 6, A x 7, E x 2, D x 6, C x 2, B x 6, A x 2,

E x 2, turn (49 blocks).

↗ **Row 66 (WS):** dec, E x 2, A x 2, B x 6, C x 2, D x 6, E x 2, A x 6, B x 2, C x 6, D x 2, E x 7, A x 6, turn (49 blocks).

Corner: start decreasing on RS.

↙ **Row 67 (RS):** dec, B x 4, A x 2, E x 6, D x 2, C x 6, B x 2, A x 7, E x 2, D x 6, C x 2, B x 6, A x 2, E x 1, turn (48 blocks).

↗ **Row 68 (WS):** dec, E x 1, A x 2, B x 6, C x 2, D x 6, E x 2, A x 6, B x 2, C x 6, D x 2, E x 7, A x 2, B x 3, turn (47 blocks).

↙ **Row 69 (RS):** dec, B x 3, A x 2, E x 6, D x 2, C x 6, B x 2, A x 7, E x 6, D x 2, C x 6, B x 2, A x 2, turn (46 blocks).

↗ **Row 70 (WS):** dec, A x 2, B x 2, C x 6, D x 2, E x 6, A x 2, B x 6, C x 2, D x 6, E x 7, A x 2, B x 2, turn (45 blocks).

↙ **Row 71 (RS):** dec, B x 2, A x 6, E x 2, D x 6, C x 2, B x 6, A x 3, E x 6, D x 2, C x 6, B x 2, A x 1, turn (44 blocks).

↗ **Row 72 (WS):** dec, A x 1, B x 2, C x 6, D x 2, E x 6, A x 2, B x 6, C x 2, D x 6, E x 3, A x 6, B x 1, turn (43 blocks).

↙ **Row 73 (RS):** dec, B x 1, A x 6, E x 2, D x 6, C x 2, B x 6, A x 7, E x 2, D x 6, C x 2, B x 2, turn (42 blocks).

↗ **Row 74 (WS):** dec, B x 2, C x 2, D x 6, E x 2, A x 6, B x 2, C x 6, D x 2, E x 7, A x 6, turn (41 blocks).

↙ **Row 75 (RS):** dec, B x 4, A x 2, E x 6, D x 2, C x 6, B x 2, A x 7, E x 2, D x 6, C x 2, B x 1, turn (40 blocks).

↗ **Row 76 (WS):** dec, B x 1, C x 2, D x 6, E x 2, A x 6, B x 2, C x 6, D x 2, E x 7, A x 2, B x 3, turn (39 blocks).

↙ **Row 77 (RS):** dec, B x 3, A x 2, E x 6, D x 2, C x 6, B x 2, A x 7, E x 6, D x 2, C x 2, turn (38 blocks).

↗ **Row 78 (WS):** dec, C x 2, D x 2, E x 6, A x 2, B x 6, C x 2, D x 6, E x 7, A x 2, B x 2, turn (37 blocks).

↙ **Row 79 (RS):** dec, B x 2, A x 6, E x 2, D x 6, C x 2, B x 6, A x 3, E x 6, D x 2, C x 1, turn (36 blocks).

↗ **Row 80 (WS):** dec, C x 1, D x 2, E x 6, A x 2, B x 6, C x 2, D x 6, E x 3, A x 6, B x 1, turn (35 blocks).

↙ **Row 81 (RS):** dec, B x 1, A x 6, E x 2, D x 6, C x 2, B x 6, A x 7, E x 2, D x 2, turn (34 blocks).

↗ **Row 82 (WS):** dec, D x 2, E x 2, A x 6, B x 2, C x 6, D x 2, E x 7, A x 6, turn (33 blocks).

↙ **Row 83 (RS):** dec, B x 4, A x 2, E x 6, D x 2, C x 6, B x 2, A x 7, E x 2, D x 1, turn (32 blocks).

↗ **Row 84 (WS):** dec, D x 1, E x 2, A x 6, B x 2, C x 6, D x 2, E x 7, A x 2, B x 3, turn (31 blocks).

↙ **Row 85 (RS):** dec, B x 3, A x 2, E x 6, D x 2, C x 6, B x 2, A x 7, E x 2, turn (30 blocks).

↗ **Row 86 (WS):** dec, E x 2, A x 2, B x 6, C x 2, D x 6, E x 7, A x 2, B x 2, turn (29 blocks).

↙ **Row 87 (RS):** dec, B x 2, A x 6, E x 2, D x 6, C x 2, B x 6, A x 3, E x 1, turn (28 blocks).

↗ **Row 88 (WS):** dec, E x 1, A x 2, B x 6, C x 2, D x 6, E x 3, A x 6, B x 1, turn (27 blocks).

↙ **Row 89 (RS):** dec, B x 1, A x 6, E x 2, D x 6, C x 2, B x 6, A x 3, turn (26 blocks).

↗ **Row 90 (WS):** dec, A x 2, B x 2, C x 6, D x 2, E x 7, A x 6, turn (25 blocks).

↙ **Row 91 (RS):** dec, B x 4, A x 2, E x 6, D x 2, C x 6, B x 2, A x 2, turn (24 blocks).

↗ **Row 92 (WS):** dec, A x 1, B x 2, C x 6, D x 2, E x 7, A x 2, B x 3, turn (23 blocks).

↙ **Row 93 (RS):** dec, B x 3, A x 2, E x 6, D x 2, C x 6, B x 2, A x 1, turn (22 blocks).

↗ **Row 94 (WS):** dec, B x 2, C x 2, D x 6, E x 7, A x 2, B x 2, turn (21 blocks).

↙ **Row 95 (RS):** dec, B x 2, A x 6, E x 2, D x 6, C x 2, B x 2, turn (20 blocks).

↗ **Row 96 (WS):** dec, B x 1, C x 2, D x 6, E x 3, A x 6, B x 1, turn (19 blocks).

↙ **Row 97 (RS):** dec, B x 1, A x 6, E x 2, D x 6, C x 2, B x 1, turn (18 blocks).

↗ **Row 98 (WS):** dec, C x 2, D x 2, E x 7, A x 6, turn (17 blocks).

↙ **Row 99 (RS):** dec, B x 4, A x 2, E x 6, D x 2, C x 2, turn (16 blocks).

↗ **Row 100 (WS):** dec, C x 1, D x 2, E x 7, A x 2, B x 3, turn (15 blocks).

↙ **Row 101 (RS):** dec, B x 3, A x 2, E x 6, D x 2, C x 1, turn (14 blocks).

↗ **Row 102 (WS):** dec, D x 2, E x 7, A x 2, B x 2, turn (13 blocks).

↙ **Row 103 (RS):** dec, B x 2, A x 6, E x 2, D x 2, turn (12 blocks).

↗ **Row 104 (WS):** dec, D x 1, E x 3, A x 6, B x 1, turn (11 blocks).

↙ **Row 105 (RS):** dec, B x 1, A x 6, E x 2, D x 1, turn (10 blocks).

↗ **Row 106 (WS):** dec, E x 3, A x 6, turn (9 blocks).

↙ **Row 107 (RS):** dec, B x 4, A x 2, E x 2, turn (8 blocks).

↗ **Row 108 (WS):** dec, E x 2, A x 2, B x 3, turn (7 blocks).

↙ **Row 109 (RS):** dec, B x 3, A x 2, E x 1, turn (6 blocks).

↗ **Row 110 (WS):** dec, E x 1, A x 2, B x 2, turn (5 blocks).

↙ **Row 111 (RS):** dec, B x 2, A x 2, turn (4 blocks).

↗ **Row 112 (WS):** dec, A x 2, B x 1, turn (3 blocks).

↙ **Row 113 (RS):** dec, B x 1, A x 1, turn (2 blocks).

↗ **Row 114 (WS):** dec, A x 1, fasten off yarn A (1 block).

Sew in all loose ends on WS of work.

Chevron Stripes

This chevron blanket is worked in strips and joined as you go. You could also use the layout chart to work the blanket in one whole piece.

SKILL LEVEL

■ ■ □

HOOK SIZE

6mm (US J-10)

BLOCK STITCH

3 tr block: (3 ch, 3 tr in ch sp)

TECHNIQUES

Join-as-you-go (see page 21)

THROW SIZE

102 x 147cm (40 x 58in)

YARN

Cascade 220® (aran/10-ply/worsted; 100g/3½oz; 200m/220yd)

■	**A**	8555 Black – 1 ball
□	**B**	8505 White – 5 balls
■	**C**	8400 Charcoal Grey – 2 balls
■	**D**	7828 Neon Yellow – 2 balls

ABBREVIATIONS & STITCHES

ch	chain
ch sp	chain space
dec	sl st in next 3 sts, sl st into 3-ch sp
inc	ch 6, 1 tr in fourth ch from hook, 1 tr in next 2 ch, sl st into ch sp of next block
rep	repeat
RS	right side
sl st	slip stitch
st(s)	stitch(es)
tr	treble crochet
WS	wrong side
↙ / ↗	direction of work

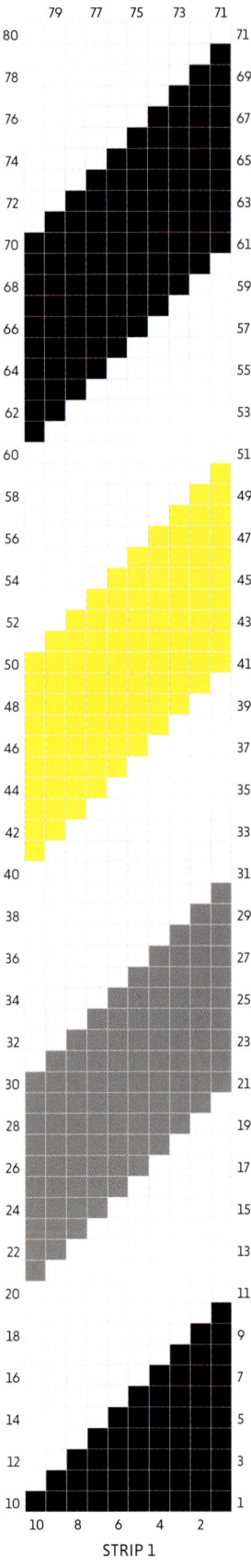

STRIP 1

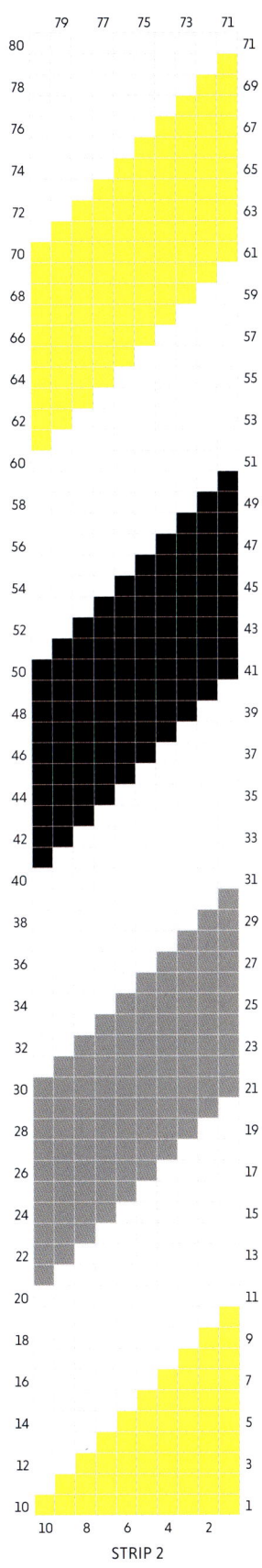

STRIP 2

Strip 1

↗ **Row 1 (WS):** using yarn A, ch 6, 1 tr in fourth ch from hook and in next 2 ch, turn (1 block).

↙ **Row 2 (RS):** inc, A x 1, turn (2 blocks).

↗ **Row 3 (WS):** inc, A x 2, turn (3 blocks).

↙ **Row 4 (RS):** inc, A x 3, turn (4 blocks).

↗ **Row 5 (WS):** inc, A x 4, turn (5 blocks).

↙ **Row 6 (RS):** inc, A x 5, turn (6 blocks).

↗ **Row 7 (WS):** inc, A x 6, turn (7 blocks).

↙ **Row 8 (RS):** inc, A x 7, turn (8 blocks).

↗ **Row 9 (WS):** inc, A x 8, turn (9 blocks).

↙ **Row 10 (RS):** inc, A x 9, turn (10 blocks).

Corner: start decreasing on WS.

↗ **Row 11 (WS):** join yarn B in 3-ch sp of last block, B x 10, turn (10 blocks).

Increase on each RS row until row 71.

↙ **Row 12 (RS):** inc, B x 9, turn (10 blocks).

↗ **Row 13 (WS):** dec, B x 10, turn (10 blocks).

Rows 14–20: rep rows 12 and 13 three times then rep row 12 once.

↗ **Row 21 (WS):** join yarn C in 3-ch sp of last block, C x 10, turn (10 blocks).

↙ **Row 22 (RS):** inc, C x 9, turn (10 blocks).

↗ **Row 23 (WS):** dec, C x 10, turn (10 blocks).

Rows 24–30: rep rows 22 and 23 three times then rep row 22 once.

1   2   3 (1)   4 (2)   5 (1)

STRIP LAYOUT CHART

↗ **Row 31 (WS):** join yarn B in 3-ch sp of last block, B x 10, turn (10 blocks).

↙ **Row 32 (RS):** inc, B x 9, turn (10 blocks).

↗ **Row 33 (WS):** dec, B x 10, turn (10 blocks).

Rows 34–40: rep rows 32 and 33 three times then rep row 32 once.

↗ **Row 41 (WS):** join yarn D in 3-ch sp, D x 10, turn (10 blocks).

↙ **Row 42 (RS):** inc, D x 9, turn (10 blocks).

↗ **Row 43 (WS):** dec, D x 10, turn (10 blocks).

Rows 44–50: rep rows 42 and 43 three times then rep row 42 once.

↗ **Row 51 (WS):** join yarn B in 3-ch sp of last block, B x 10, turn (10 blocks).

↙ **Row 52 (RS):** inc, B x 9, turn (10 blocks).

↗ **Row 53 (WS):** dec, B x 10, turn (10 blocks).

Rows 54–60: rep rows 52 and 53 three times then rep row 52 once.

↗ **Row 61 (WS):** join yarn A in 3-ch sp, A x 10, turn (10 blocks).

↙ **Row 62 (RS):** inc, A x 9, turn (10 blocks).

↗ **Row 63 (WS):** dec, A x 10, turn (10 blocks).

Rows 64–70: rep rows 62 and 63 three times then rep row 62 once.

↗ **Row 71 (WS):** join yarn B in 3-ch sp, B x 10, turn (10 blocks).

Corner: start decreasing at both edges.

↙ **Row 72 (RS):** dec, B x 9, turn (9 blocks).

↗ **Row 73 (WS):** dec, B x 8, turn (8 blocks).

↙ **Row 74 (RS):** dec, B x 7, turn (7 blocks).

↗ **Row 75 (WS):** dec, B x 6, turn (6 blocks).

↙ **Row 76 (RS):** dec, B x 5, turn (5 blocks).

↗ **Row 77 (WS):** dec, B x 4, turn (4 blocks).

↙ **Row 78 (RS):** dec, B x 3, turn (3 blocks).

↗ **Row 79 (WS):** dec, B x 2, turn (2 blocks).

↙ **Row 80 (RS):** dec, B x 1 (1 block).

Sew in all loose ends on WS of work.

Strip 2

Join Strip 2 to Strip 1 as you go.

Beginning join: using yarn D, join to top left corner of Strip 1 with RS facing, 3 ch, sl st into next ch sp between two blocks, turn.

↗ **Row 1 (WS):** D x 1, turn (1 block).

↙ **Row 2 (RS):** inc, D x 2, sl st in next gap on Strip 1, 3 ch, sl st in next gap on Strip 1, turn (2 blocks).

↗ **Row 3 (WS):** D x 3, turn (3 blocks).

↙ **Row 4 (RS):** inc, D x 3, sl st in next gap on Strip 1, 3 ch, sl st in next gap on Strip 1, turn (4 blocks).

↗ **Row 5 (WS):** D x 5, turn (5 blocks).

↙ **Row 6 (RS):** inc, D x 5, sl st in next gap on Strip 1, 3 ch, sl st in next gap on Strip 1, turn (6 blocks).

↗ **Row 7 (WS):** D x 6, turn (7 blocks).

↙ **Row 8 (RS):** inc, D x 8, sl st in next gap on Strip 1, 3 ch, sl st in next gap on Strip 1, turn (8 blocks).

↗ **Row 9 (WS):** D x 9, turn (9 blocks).

↙ **Row 10 (RS):** inc, D x 9 changing to yarn B when working last st, now working in B sl st in next gap on Strip 1, 3 ch, sl st in next gap on Strip 1 (10 blocks).

Start decreasing on RS. Increase on each WS row until row 71.

↗ **Row 11 (WS):** inc, B x 9, turn (10 blocks).

↙ **Row 12 (RS):** dec, B x 10, sl st in next gap on Strip 1, 3 ch, sl st in next gap on Strip 1, turn (10 blocks).

Rows 13–20: rep rows 11 and 12 four times changing to yarn C when working last tr.

↗ **Row 21 (WS):** inc, C x 9, turn (10 blocks).

↙ **Row 22 (RS):** dec, C x 10, sl st in next gap on Strip 1, 3 ch, sl st in next gap on Strip 1, turn (10 blocks).

Rows 23–30: rep rows 21 and 22 four times changing to yarn B when working last tr.

↗ **Row 31 (WS):** inc, B x 9, turn (10 blocks).

↙ **Row 32 (RS):** dec, B x 10, sl st in next gap on Strip 1, 3 ch, sl st in next gap on Strip 1, turn (10 blocks).

Rows 33–40: rep rows 31 and 32 four times, changing to yarn A when working last tr.

↗ **Row 41 (WS):** inc, A x 9, turn (10 blocks).

↙ **Row 42 (RS):** dec, A x 10, sl st in next gap on Strip 1, 3 ch, sl st in next gap on Strip 1, turn (10 blocks).

Rows 43–50: rep rows 41 and 42 four times changing to yarn B when working last tr.

↗ **Row 51 (WS):** inc, B x 9, turn (10 blocks).

↙ **Row 52 (RS):** dec, B x 10, sl st in next gap on Strip 1, 3 ch, sl st in next gap on Strip 1, turn (10 blocks).

Rows 53–60: rep rows 51 and 52 four times changing to yarn D when working last tr.

↗ **Row 61 (WS):** inc, D x 9, turn (10 blocks).

↙ **Row 62 (RS):** dec, D x 10, sl st in next gap on Strip 1, 3 ch, sl st in next gap on Strip 1, turn (10 blocks).

Rows 63–70: rep rows 61 and 62 four times changing to yarn B when working last tr.

Corner: start decreasing at both edges.

↗ **Row 71 (WS):** dec, B x 10, turn (10 blocks).

↙ **Row 72 (RS):** dec, B x 9, turn (9 blocks).

↗ **Row 73 (WS):** dec, B x 8, turn (8 blocks).

↙ **Row 74 (RS):** dec, B x 7, turn (7 blocks).

↗ **Row 75 (WS):** dec, B x 6, turn (6 blocks).

↙ **Row 76 (RS):** dec, B x 5, turn (5 blocks).

↗ **Row 77 (WS):** dec, B x 4, turn (4 blocks).

↙ **Row 78 (RS):** dec, B x 3, turn (3 blocks).

↗ **Row 79 (WS):** dec, B x 2, turn (2 blocks).

↙ **Row 80 (RS):** dec, B x 1 (1 block).

Sew in all loose ends on WS of work.

Strip 3

Join Strip 3 to Strip 2 as you go.

Beginning join: using yarn A, join in the bottom left corner of Strip 1 with WS facing, 3 ch, sl st into next ch sp between two blocks, turn.

↙ Row 1 (RS): A x 1, turn (1 block).

↗ Row 2 (WS): inc, A x 1, sl st in next gap on Strip 2, 3 ch, sl st in next gap on Strip 2, turn (2 blocks).

↙ Row 3 (RS): A x 3, turn (3 blocks).

↗ Row 4 (WS): inc, A x 3, sl st in next gap on Strip 2, 3 ch, sl st in next gap on Strip 2, turn (4 blocks).

↙ Row 5 (RS): A x 5, turn (5 blocks).

↗ Row 6 (WS): inc, A x 5, sl st in next gap on Strip 2, 3 ch, sl st in next gap on Strip 2, turn (6 blocks).

↙ Row 7 (RS): A x 7, turn (7 blocks).

↗ Row 8 (WS): inc, A x 7, sl st in next gap on Strip 2, 3 ch, sl st in next gap on Strip 2, turn (8 blocks).

↙ Row 9 (RS): A x 9, turn (9 blocks).

↗ Row 10 (WS): inc, A x 9 changing to yarn B when working last tr, sl st in next gap on Strip 2, 3 ch, sl st in next gap on Strip 2, turn (10 blocks).

Start decreasing on WS. Increase on RS rows.

↙ Row 11 (RS): inc, B x 9, turn (10 blocks).

↗ Row 12 (WS): dec, B x 10, sl st in next gap on Strip 2, 3 ch, sl st in next gap on Strip 2, turn (10 blocks).

Rows 13–20: rep rows 11 and 12 four times changing to yarn C when working last tr.

↙ Row 21 (RS): inc, C x 9, turn (10 blocks).

↗ Row 22 (WS): dec, C x 10, sl st in next gap on Strip 2, 3 ch, sl st in next gap on Strip 2, turn (10 blocks).

Row 23–30: rep rows 21 and 22 four times changing to yarn B when working last tr.

↙ Row 31 (RS): inc, B x 9, turn (10 blocks).

↗ Row 32 (WS): dec, B x 10, sl st in next gap on Strip 2, 3 ch, sl st in next gap on Strip 2, turn (10 blocks).

Rows 33–40: rep rows 31 and 32 four times changing to yarn D when working last tr.

↙ Row 41 (RS): inc, D x 9, turn (10 blocks).

↗ Row 42 (WS): dec, D x 10, sl st in next gap on Strip 2, 3 ch, sl st in next gap on Strip 2, turn (10 blocks).

Rows 43–50: rep rows 41 and 42 four times changing to yarn B when working last tr.

↙ Row 51 (RS): inc, B x 9, turn (10 blocks).

↗ Row 52 (WS): dec, B x 10, sl st in next gap on Strip 2, 3 ch, sl st in next gap on Strip 2 (10 blocks).

Rows 53–60: rep rows 51 and 52 four times changing to yarn A when working last tr.

↙ Row 61 (RS): inc, A x 9 (10 squares).

↗ Row 62 (WS): dec, A x 10, sl st in next gap on Strip 2, 3 ch, sl st in next gap on Strip 2, turn (10 blocks).

Rows 63–70: rep rows 61 and 62 four times changing to yarn B when working last tr.

Corner: start decreasing at both edges.

↙ Row 71 (RS): dec, B x 10, turn (10 blocks).

↗ Row 72 (WS): dec, B x 9, turn (9 blocks).

↙ Row 73 (RS): dec, B x 8, turn (8 blocks).

↗ Row 74 (WS): dec, B x 7, turn (7 blocks).

↙ Row 75 (RS): dec, B x 6, turn (6 blocks).

↗ Row 76 (WS): dec, B x 5, turn (5 blocks).

↙ Row 77 (RS): dec, B x 4, turn (4 blocks).

↗ Row 78 (WS): dec, B x 3, turn (3 blocks).

↙ Row 79 (RS): dec, B x 2, turn (2 blocks).

↗ Row 80 (WS): dec, B x 1, turn (1 block).

Sew in all loose ends on WS of work.

Throw

Rep Strip 2 joining it to Strip 3 as you go.
Then rep Strip 1 joining it to Strip 4 as you go.
Sew in all loose ends on WS of work.

Crosses

This throw is great for using up leftover yarn from other projects by working each cross in a different colour. Alternatively, you could work all of the crosses in the same colour for a simple and stylish throw.

SKILL LEVEL

◻ ◻ ◻

HOOK SIZE

6mm (US J-10)

BLOCK STITCH

3 tr block: (3 ch, 3 tr in ch sp)

THROW SIZE

110 x 160cm (43¼ x 63in)

YARN

Cascade 220® (aran/10-ply/worsted; 100g/3½oz; 200m/220yd)

	A	1058 Nimbus Cloud – 9 balls
	B	1057 Peony – 1 ball
	C	1072 Key West – 1 ball
	D	1073 Water Spout – 1 ball
	E	1070 Golden Kiwi – 1 ball

Number of bobbins

B x 6, C x 6, D x 6, E x 6

ABBREVIATIONS & STITCHES

ch	chain
ch sp	chain space
dec	sl st in next 3 sts, sl st into 3-ch sp
inc	ch 6, 1 tr in fourth ch from hook, 1 tr in next 2 ch, sl st into ch sp of next block
NB	join in new bobbin
RB	remove bobbin and cut yarn
rep	repeat
RS	right side
sl st	slip stitch
st(s)	stitch(es)
tr	treble crochet
WS	wrong side
↙ / ↗	direction of work

NOTE

Carry yarn A when not in use by working your stitches over the carried yarn.

Throw

↙ Row 1 (RS): using yarn A, ch 6, 1 tr in fourth ch from hook, 1 tr in next 2 ch (1 block).

↗ Row 2 (WS): inc, A x 1, turn (2 blocks).

↙ Row 3 (RS): inc, A x 2, turn (3 blocks).

↗ Row 4 (WS): inc, A x 3, turn (4 blocks).

↙ Row 5 (RS): inc, A x 4, turn (5 blocks).

↗ Row 6 (WS): inc, A x 5, turn (6 blocks).

↙ Row 7 (RS): inc, A x 6, turn (7 blocks).

↗ Row 8 (WS): inc, A x 7, turn (8 blocks).

↙ Row 9 (RS): inc, A x 2, B x 1, A x 2, B x 1, A x 2, turn (9 blocks).

↗ Row 10 (WS): inc, A x 1, B x 2, A x 1, B x 2, A x 3, turn (10 blocks).

↙ Row 11 (RS): inc, A x 2, B x 6, A x 2, turn (11 blocks).

↗ Row 12 (WS): inc, A x 2, B x 5, A x 4, turn (12 blocks).

↙ Row 13 (RS): inc, A x 4, B x 4, A x 4, turn (13 blocks).

↗ Row 14 (WS): inc, A x 4, B x 3, A x 6, turn (14 blocks).

↙ Row 15 (RS): inc, A x 4, B x 4, A x 5, turn (15 blocks).

↗ Row 16 (WS): inc, A x 4, B x 5, A x 6, turn (16 blocks).

↙ Row 17 (RS): inc, A x 5, B x 6, A x 5, turn (17 blocks).

↗ Row 18 (WS): inc, A x 5, B x 2, A x 1, B x 2, A x 7, turn (18 blocks).

↙ Row 19 (RS): inc, A x 7, B x 1, A x 2, B x 1, A x 7, fasten off yarn B, turn (19 blocks).

↗ Row 20 (WS): inc, A x 19, turn (20 blocks).

↙ Row 21 (RS): inc, A x 20, turn (21 blocks).

↗ Row 22 (WS): inc, A x 1, C x 1, A x 2, C x 1, A x 9, C x 1, A x 2, C x 1, A x 3, turn (22 blocks).

↙ Row 23 (RS): inc, A x 2, C x 2, A x 1, C x 2, A x 8, C x 2, A x 1, C x 2, A x 2, turn (23 blocks).

↗ Row 24 (WS): inc, A x 1, C x 6, A x 7, C x 6, A x 3, turn (24 blocks).

↙ Row 25 (RS): inc, A x 3, C x 5, A x 8, C x 5, A x 3, turn (25 blocks).

↗ Row 26 (WS): inc, A x 3, C x 4, A x 9, C x 4, A x 5, turn (26 blocks).

↙ Row 27 (RS): inc, A x 5, C x 3, A x 10, C x 3, A x 5, turn (27 blocks).

↗ Row 28 (WS): inc, A x 4, C x 4, A x 9, C x 4, A x 6, turn (28 blocks).

↙ Row 29 (RS): inc, A x 5, C x 5, A x 8, C x 5, A x 5, turn (29 blocks).

↗ Row 30 (WS): inc, A x 4, C x 6, A x 7, C x 6, A x 6, turn (30 blocks).

↙ Row 31 (RS): inc, A x 6, C x 2, A x 1, C x 2, A x 8, C x 2, A x 1, C x 2, A x 6, turn (31 blocks).

↗ Row 32 (WS): inc, A x 6, C x 1, A x 2, C x 1, A x 9, C x 1, A x 2, C x 1, A x 8, fasten off yarn C, turn (32 blocks).

↙ Row 33 (RS): inc, A x 32, turn (33 blocks).

↗ Row 34 (WS): inc, A x 33, turn (34 blocks).

↙ Row 35 (RS): inc, A x 2, B x 1, A x 2, B x 1, A x 9, D x 1, A x 2, D x 1, A x 9, E x 1, A x 2, E x 1, A x 2, turn (35 blocks).

↗ Row 36 (WS): inc, A x 1, E x 2, A x 1, E x 2, A x 8, D x 2, A x 1, D x 2, A x 8, B x 2, A x 1, B x 2, A x 3, turn (36 blocks).

↙ Row 37 (RS): inc, A x 2, B x 6, A x 7, D x 6, A x 7, E x 6, A x 2, turn (37 blocks).

↗ Row 38 (WS): inc, A x 2, E x 5, A x 8, D x 5, A x 8, B x 5, A x 4, turn (38 blocks).

↙ Row 39 (RS): inc, A x 4, B x 4, A x 9, D x 4, A x 9, E x 4, A x 4, turn (39 blocks).

↗ Row 40 (WS): inc, A x 4, E x 3, A x 10, D x 3, A x 10, B x 3, A x 6, turn (40 blocks).

↙ Row 41 (RS): inc, A x 5, B x 4, A x 9, D x 4, A x 9, E x 4, A x 5, turn (41 blocks).

↗ Row 42 (WS): inc, A x 4, E x 5, A x 8, D x 5, A x 8, B x 5, A x 6, turn (42 blocks).

↙ Row 43 (RS): inc, A x 5, B x 6, A x 7, D x 6, A x 7, E x 6, A x 5, turn (43 blocks).

↗ Row 44 (WS): inc, A x 5, E x 2, A x 1, E x 2, A x 8, D x 2, A x 1, D x 2, A x 8, B x 2, A x 1, B x 2, A x 7, turn (44 blocks).

↙ Row 45 (RS): inc, A x 7, B x 1, A x 2, B x 1, A x 9, D x 1, A x 2, D x 1, A x 9, E x 1, A x 2, E x 1, A x 7, fasten off yarns B and D, turn (45 blocks).

↗ Row 46 (WS): inc, A x 45, turn (46 blocks).

↙ Row 47 (RS): inc, A x 46, turn (47 blocks).

↗ Row 48 (WS): inc, A x 1, D x 1, A x 2, D x 1, A x 9, B x 1, A x 2, B x 1, A x 9, E x 1, A x 2, E x 1, A x 9, C x 1, A x 2, C x 1, A x 3, turn (48 blocks).

↙ Row 49 (RS): inc, A x 2, C x 2, A x 1, C x 2, A x 8, E x 2, A x 1, E x 2, A x 8, B x 2, A x 1, B x 2, A x 8, D x 2, A x 1, D x 2, A x 2, turn (49 blocks).

↗ Row 50 (WS): inc, A x 1, D x 6, A x 7, B x 6, A x 7, E x 6, A x 7, C x 6, A x 3, turn (50 blocks).

↙ Row 51 (RS): inc, A x 3, C x 5, A x 8, E x 5, A x 8, B x 5, A x 8, D x 5, A x 3, turn (51 blocks).

↗ Row 52 (WS): inc, A x 3, D x 4, A x 9, B x 4, A x 9, E x 4, A x 9, C x 4, A x 5, turn (52 blocks).

↙ Row 53 (RS): inc, A x 5, C x 3, A x 10, E x 3, A x 10, B x 3, A x 10, D x 3, A x 5, turn (53 blocks).

↗ Row 54 (WS): inc, A x 4, D x 4, A x 9, B x 4, A x 9, E x 4, A x 9, C x 4, A x 6, turn (54 blocks).

Corner: start decreasing on WS.

↙ Row 55 (RS): inc, A x 6, C x 5, A x 8, E x 5, A x 8, B x 5, A x 8, D x 5, A x 4, turn (54 blocks).

↗ Row 56 (WS): dec, A x 2, D x 6, A x 7, B x 6, A x 7, E x 6, A x 7, C x 6, A x 6, turn (54 blocks).

↙ Row 57 (RS): inc, A x 7, C x 2, A x 1, C x 2, A x 8, E x 2, A x 1, E x 2, A x 8, B x 2, A x 1, B x 2, A x 8, D x 2, A x 1, D x 2, A x 3, turn (54 blocks).

↗ Row 58 (WS): dec, A x 2, D x 1, A x 2, D x 1, A x 9, B x 1, A x 2, B x 1, A x 9, E x 1, A x 2, E x 1, A x 9, C x 1, A x 2, C x 1, A x 8, fasten off yarns D, B, E, and C, turn (54 blocks).

↙ Row 59 (RS): inc, A x 54, turn (54 blocks).

↗ Row 60 (WS): dec, A x 53, turn (54 blocks).

↙ Row 61 (RS): inc, A x 3, D x 1, A x 2, D x 1, A x 9, B x 1, A x 2, B x 1, A x 9, C x 1, A x 2, C x 1, A x 9, E x 1, A x 2, E x 1, A x 8, turn (54 blocks).

↗ Row 62 (WS): dec, A x 6, E x 2, A x 1, E x 2, A x 8, C x 2, A x 1, C x 2, A x 8, B x 2, A x 1, B x 2, A x 8, D x 2, A x 1, D x 2, A x 3, turn (54 blocks).

↙ Row 63 (RS): inc, A x 3, D x 6, A x 7, B x 6, A x 7, C x 6, A x 7, E x 6, A x 6, turn (54 blocks).

↗ Row 64 (WS): dec, A x 5, E x 5, A x 8, C x 5, A x 8, B x 5, A x 8, D x 5, A x 4, turn (54 blocks).

↙ Row 65 (RS): inc, A x 5, D x 4, A x 9, B x 4, A x 9, C x 4, A x 9, E x 4, A x 6, turn (54 blocks).

↗ Row 66 (WS): dec, A x 5, E x 3, A x 10, C x 3, A x 10, B x 3, A x 10, D x 3, A x 6, turn (54 blocks).

↙ Row 67 (RS): inc, A x 6, D x 4, A x 9, B x 4, A x 9, C x 4, A x 9, E x 4, A x 5, turn (54 blocks).

↗ Row 68 (WS): dec, A x 3, E x 5, A x 8,

C x 5, A x 8, B x 5, A x 8, D x 5, A x 6, turn (54 blocks).

↙ Row 69 (RS): inc, A x 6, D x 6, A x 7, B x 6, A x 7, C x 6, A x 7, E x 6, A x 3, turn (54 blocks).

↗ Row 70 (WS): dec, A x 2, E x 2, A x 1, E x 2, A x 8, C x 2, A x 1, C x 2, A x 8, B x 2, A x 1, B x 2, A x 8, D x 2, A x 1, D x 2, A x 7, turn (54 blocks).

↙ Row 71 (RS): inc, A x 8, D x 1, A x 2, D x 1, A x 9, B x 1, A x 2, B x 1, A x 9, C x 1, A x 2, C x 1, A x 9, E x 1, A x 2, E x 1, A x 3, fasten off yarns D, B, C, and E, turn (54 blocks).

↗ Row 72 (WS): dec, A x 53, turn (54 blocks).

↙ Row 73 (RS): inc, A x 54, turn (54 blocks).

↗ Row 74 (WS): dec, A x 7, D x 1, A x 2, D x 1, A x 9, D x 1, A x 2, D x 1, A x 9, C x 1, A x 2, C x 1, A x 9, E x 1, A x 2, E x 1, A x 3, turn (54 blocks).

↙ Row 75 (RS): inc, A x 3, E x 2, A x 1, E x 2, A x 8, C x 2, A x 1, C x 2, A x 8, D x 2, A x 1, D x 2, A x 8, D x 2, A x 1, D x 2, A x 7, turn (54 blocks).

↗ Row 76 (WS): dec, A x 5, D x 6, A x 7, D x 6, A x 7, C x 6, A x 7, E x 6, A x 3, turn (54 blocks).

↙ Row 77 (RS): inc, A x 4, E x 5, A x 8, C x 5, A x 8, D x 5, A x 8, D x 5, A x 6, turn (54 blocks).

↗ Row 78 (WS): dec, A x 5, D x 4, A x 9, D x 4, A x 9, C x 4, A x 9, E x 4, A x 5, turn (54 blocks).

Corner: start decreasing on RS.

↙ Row 79 (RS): dec, A x 5, E x 3, A x 10, C x 3, A x 10, D x 3, A x 10, D x 3, A x 6, turn (53 blocks).

↗ Row 80 (WS): dec, A x 5, D x 4, A x 9, D x 4, A x 9, C x 4, A x 9, E x 4, A x 4, turn (52 blocks).

↙ Row 81 (RS): dec, A x 3, E x 5, A x 8, C x 5, A x 8, D x 5, A x 8, D x 5, A x 4, turn (51 blocks).

↗ Row 82 (WS): dec, A x 3, D x 6, A x 7, D x 6, A x 7, C x 6, A x 7, E x 6, A x 2, turn (50 blocks).

↙ Row 83 (RS): dec, A x 2, E x 2, A x 1, E x 2, A x 8, C x 2, A x 1, C x 2, A x 8, D x 2, A x 1, D x 2, A x 8, D x 2, A x 1, D x 2, A x 3, turn (49 blocks).

↗ Row 84 (WS): dec, A x 3, D x 1, A x 2, D x 1,

A x 9, D x 1, A x 2, D x 1, A x 9, C x 1, A x 2, C x 1, A x 9, E x 1, A x 2, E x 1, A x 2, fasten off yarns D, C, and E, turn (48 blocks).

↙ Row 85 (RS): dec, A x 47, turn (47 blocks).

↗ Row 86 (WS): dec, A x 46, turn (46 blocks).

↙ Row 87 (RS): dec, A x 7, D x 1, A x 2, D x 1, A x 9, E x 1, A x 2, E x 1, A x 9, E x 1, A x 2, E x 1, A x 8, turn (45 blocks).

↗ Row 88 (WS): dec, A x 7, E x 2, A x 1, E x 2, A x 8, E x 2, A x 1, E x 2, A x 8, D x 2, A x 1, D x 2, A x 6, turn (44 blocks).

↙ Row 89 (RS): dec, A x 5, D x 6, A x 7, E x 6, A x 7, E x 6, A x 6, turn (43 blocks).

↗ Row 90 (WS): dec, A x 6, E x 5, A x 8, E x 5, A x 8, D x 5, A x 5, turn (42 blocks).

↙ Row 91 (RS): dec, A x 5, D x 4, A x 9, E x 4, A x 9, E x 4, A x 6, turn (41 blocks).

↗ Row 92 (WS): dec, A x 6, E x 3, A x 10, E x 3, A x 10, D x 3, A x 5, turn (40 blocks).

↙ Row 93 (RS): dec, A x 4, D x 4, A x 9, E x 4, A x 9, E x 4, A x 5, turn (39 blocks).

↗ Row 94 (WS): dec, A x 4, E x 5, A x 8, E x 5, A x 8, D x 5, A x 3, turn (38 blocks).

↙ Row 95 (RS): dec, A x 2, D x 6, A x 7, E x 6, A x 7, E x 6, A x 3, turn (37 blocks).

↗ Row 96 (WS): dec, A x 3, E x 2, A x 1, E x 2, A x 8, E x 2, A x 1, E x 2, A x 8, D x 2, A x 1, D x 2, A x 2, turn (36 blocks).

↙ Row 97 (RS): dec, A x 2, D x 1, A x 2, D x 1, A x 9, E x 1, A x 2, E x 1, A x 9, E x 1, A x 2, E x 1, A x 3, fasten off yarns D and E, turn (35 blocks).

↗ Row 98 (WS): dec, A x 34, turn (34 blocks).

↙ Row 99 (RS): dec, A x 33, turn (33 blocks).

↗ Row 100 (WS): dec, A x 8, B x 1, A x 2, B x 1, A x 9, B x 1, A x 2, B x 1, A x 7, turn (32 blocks).

↙ Row 101 (RS): dec, A x 6, B x 2, A x 1, B x 2, A x 8, B x 2, A x 1, B x 2, A x 7, turn (31 blocks).

↙ Row 102 (WS): dec, A x 6, B x 6, A x 7, B x 6, A x 5, turn (30 blocks).

↙ Row 103 (RS): dec, A x 5, B x 5, A x 8, B x 5, A x 6, turn (29 blocks).

↗ Row 104 (WS): dec, A x 6, B x 4, A x 9, B x 4, A x 5, turn (28 blocks).

↙ Row 105 (RS): dec, A x 5, B x 3, A x 10, B x 3, A x 6, turn (27 blocks).

↗ Row 106 (WS): dec, A x 5, B x 4, A x 9, B x 4, A x 4, turn (26 blocks).

↙ Row 107 (RS): dec, A x 3, B x 5, A x 8, B x 5, A x 4, turn (25 blocks).

↗ Row 108 (WS): dec, A x 3, B x 6, A x 7, B x 6, A x 2, turn (24 blocks).

↙ Row 109 (RS): dec, A x 2, B x 2, A x 1, B x 2, A x 8, B x 2, A x 1, B x 2, A x 3, turn (23 blocks).

↗ Row 110 (WS): dec, A x 3, B x 1, A x 2, B x 1, A x 9, B x 1, A x 2, B x 1, A x 2, fasten off yarn B, turn (22 blocks).

↙ Row 111 (RS): dec, A x 21, turn (21 blocks).

↙ Row 112 (WS): dec, A x 20, turn (20 blocks).

↙ Row 113 (RS): dec, A x 7, C x 1, A x 2, C x 1, A x 8, turn (19 blocks).

↗ Row 114 (WS): dec, A x 7, C x 2, A x 1, C x 2, A x 6, turn (18 blocks).

↙ Row 115 (RS): dec, A x 5, C x 6, A x 6, turn (17 blocks).

↗ Row 116 (WS): dec, A x 6, C x 5, A x 5, turn (16 blocks).

↙ Row 117 (RS): dec, A x 5, C x 4, A x 6, turn (15 blocks).

↗ Row 118 (WS): dec, A x 6, C x 3, A x 5, turn (14 blocks).

↙ Row 119 (RS): dec, A x 4, C x 4, A x 5, turn (13 blocks).

↗ Row 120 (WS): dec, A x 4, C x 5, A x 3, turn (12 blocks).

↙ Row 121 (RS): dec, A x 2, C x 6, A x 3, turn (11 blocks).

↗ Row 122 (WS): dec, A x 3, C x 2, A x 1, C x 2, A x 2, turn (10 blocks).

↙ Row 123 (RS): dec, A x 2, C x 1, A x 2, C x 1, A x 3, fasten off yarn C, turn (9 blocks).

↗ Row 124 (WS): dec, A x 8, turn (8 blocks).

↙ Row 125 (RS): dec, A x 7, turn (7 blocks).

↗ Row 126 (WS): dec, A x 6, turn (6 blocks).

↙ Row 127 (RS): dec, A x 5, turn (5 blocks).

↗ Row 128 (WS): dec, A x 4, turn (4 blocks).

↙ Row 129 (RS): dec, A x 3, turn (3 blocks).

↗ Row 130 (WS): dec, A x 2, turn (2 blocks).

↙ Row 131 (RS): dec, A x 1, fasten off yarn A (1 block).

Sew in all loose ends on WS of work.

Striped Corners

This geometric blanket is created by crocheting individual squares that are joined together at the end. You can create a different look by laying out the completed blocks in different patterns. A neat edging makes this block very versatile.

SKILL LEVEL

☐ ☐ ☐

HOOK SIZE

6mm (US J-10)

BLOCK STITCH

3 tr block: (3 ch, 3 tr in ch sp)

TECHNIQUES

Join-as-you-go (see page 21)

SQUARE SIZE

28 x 28cm (11 x 11in)

THROW SIZE

112 x 168cm (44 x 66in)

YARN

Cascade 220® (aran/10-ply/worsted; 100g/3½oz; 200m/220yd)

	A	1049 Peach Dust – 4 balls
	B	8505 White – 4 balls
	C	1050 Harbor Mist – 4 balls
	D	1073 Water Spout – 4 balls

Yarn per square:

	A	51m (56yd)
	B	27m (30yd)
	C	17m (19yd)
	D	51m (56yd)

ABBREVIATIONS & STITCHES

ch	chain
ch sp	chain space
dc	double crochet
dec	sl st in next 3 sts, sl st into 3-ch sp
inc	ch 6, 1 tr in fourth ch from hook, 1 tr in next 2 ch, sl st into ch sp of next block
RS	right side
sl st	slip stitch
st(s)	stitch(es)
tr	treble crochet
WS	wrong side
[ ]	repeat instructions between brackets number of times stated
*/**	repeat instructions following asterisk/between asterisks as directed
↙/↗	direction of work

SQUARE LAYOUT CHART

Square

Make 24 squares.

↙ Row 1 (RS): using yarn A, 6 ch, 1 tr in fourth ch from hook, 1 tr in next 2 ch, turn (1 block).

↗ Row 2 (WS): inc, A x 1, turn (2 blocks).

↙ Row 3 (RS): inc, A x 2, turn (3 blocks).

↗ Row 4 (WS): inc, A x 3, turn (4 blocks).

↙ Row 5 (RS): inc, A x 4, turn (5 blocks).

↗ Row 6 (WS): inc, A x 5, turn (6 blocks).

↙ Row 7 (RS): inc, A x 6, turn (7 blocks).

↗ Row 8 (WS): inc, A x 7, turn (8 blocks).

↙ Row 9 (RS): inc, A x 8, turn (9 blocks).

↗ Row 10 (WS): inc, A x 9, turn (10 blocks).

↙ Row 11 (RS): inc, A x 10, turn (11 blocks).

↗ Row 12 (WS): inc, A x 11, turn (12 blocks).

↙ Row 13 (RS): inc, A x 12, fasten off yarn A, turn (13 blocks).

Corner: start decreasing at both ends.

↗ Row 14 (WS): join yarn B in last ch sp made, B x 12, turn (12 blocks).

↙ Row 15 (RS): dec, B x 11, turn (11 blocks).

↗ Row 16 (WS): dec, B x 10, fasten off yarn B, turn (10 blocks).

↙ Row 17 (RS): join yarn C in last ch sp made, C x 9, turn (9 blocks).

↗ Row 18 (WS): dec, C x 8, turn (8 blocks).

↙ Row 19 (RS): dec, C x 7, turn (7 blocks).

↗ Row 20 (WS): join yarn B in last ch sp made, B x 6, turn (6 blocks).

↙ Row 21 (RS): dec, B x 5, turn (5 blocks).

↗ Row 22 (WS): dec, B x 4, fasten off yarn B, turn (4 blocks).

↙ Row 23 (RS): join yarn C in last ch sp made, C x 3, turn (3 blocks).

↗ Row 24 (WS): dec, C x 2, turn (2 blocks).

↙ Row 25 (RS): dec, C x 1, turn (1 block).

Edging

↙ Row 1 (RS): join yarn A or D in first st of first block in matching colour in the bottom left of the square, 1 ch, 1 dc in next 2 sts, 3 dc in corner, [2 dc in side of st, 1 dc in each of next 3 sts] six times, work another 2 sts in same place as last st made, * 2 dc in side of next st changing to yarn B when working last st, now in B 1 dc in next 3 sts, 2 dc in side of next st, 1 dc in 3 sts changing to yarn C when working last st, now in C work from * once, changing to yarn B when working last st, repeat from * in B** changing to yarn C when working last st, 2 dc in side of next st, 1 dc in 3 sts, 2 dc in side of next st, 3 dc in corner, repeat from * to ** once, join to first st made. Fasten off all yarn colours.

Sew in all loose ends on WS of work.

Throw

Joining

Following the layout chart, sew the squares together in 6 rows of 4 squares. Use any colour and the invisible seam method. Sew in all loose ends on WS of work.

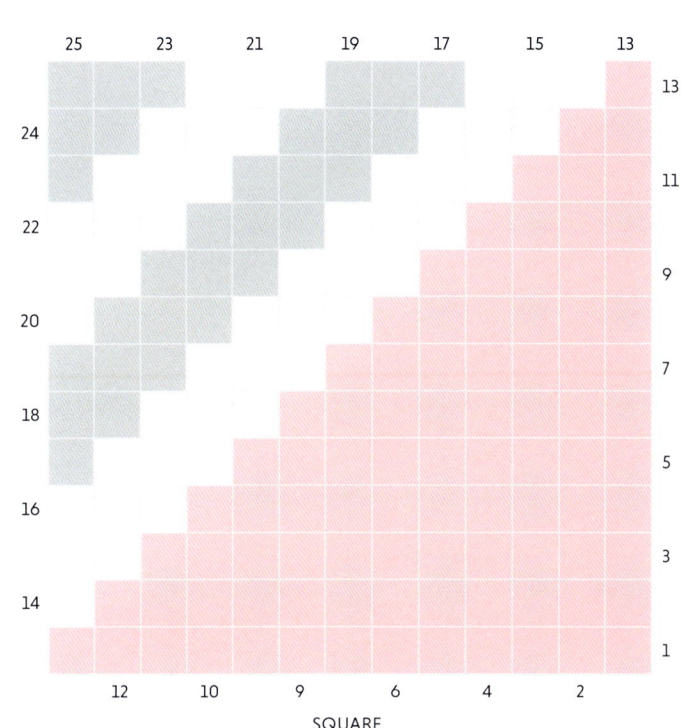

Diamond Tiles

This throw is created by working join-as-you-go squares. Each square features a diamond motif at the center, and the corners of the squares create more diamond motifs when joined. This is a great project to tackle one square at a time. You could also use the square pattern to make a cushion cover. If you would like a larger throw, use the yarn requirements for one square to calculate how much extra yarn you'll need.

SKILL LEVEL

□ □ □

HOOK SIZE

4mm (US G-6)

BLOCK STITCH

3 tr block: (3 ch, 3 tr in ch sp)

TECHNIQUES

Join-as-you-go (see page 21)
Colour changes (see page 22)

SQUARE SIZE

30 x 30cm (12 x 12in)

THROW SIZE

90 x 120cm (35½ x 47¼in)

YARN

Cascade 220 Superwash® (DK/8-ply/light worsted; 100g/3½oz; 200m/220yd)

□	A	871 White – 6 balls
■	B	811 Como Blue – 1 ball
■	C	1960 Pacific – 1 ball
■	D	259 Blue Turquoise – 1 ball
■	E	288 Green Spruce – 1 ball
■	F	886 Citron – 1 ball
■	G	821 Daffodil – 1 ball

Yarn per square

□	A	88m (96yd)
■	B	57m (62yd)

Number of bobbins

A x 7, B x 6, C x 6, D x 6, E x 6, F x 6, G x 6

ABBREVIATIONS & STITCHES

ch	chain
ch sp	chain space
dec	sl st in next 3 sts, sl st into 3-ch sp
inc	ch 6, 1 tr in fourth ch from hook, 1 tr in next 2 ch, sl st into ch sp of next block
NB	join in new bobbin
RB	remove bobbin and cut yarn
RS	right side
sl st	slip stitch
st(s)	stitch(es)
tr	treble crochet
WS	wrong side
↙/↗	direction of work

37 35 33 31 29 27 25 23 21 19

36

34

32

30

28

26

24

22

20

19

17

15

13

11

9

7

5

3

1

18 16 14 12 10 8 6 4 2

SQUARE

SQUARE LAYOUT CHART

Square

Make 1 square in the following colourway. Make a further 11 squares, one in each of the colours C–G, and join-as-you-go, following the layout chart. Make a total of 12 squares.

↙ **Row 1 (RS):** using yarn A, ch 6, 1 tr in fourth ch from hook and in next 2 ch, turn (1 block).

↗ **Row 2 (WS):** inc, A x 1, fasten off yarn A, turn (2 blocks).

↙ **Row 3 (RS):** join yarn B, inc, B x 2, turn (3 blocks).

↗ **Row 4 (WS):** inc, B x 3, fasten off yarn B, turn (4 blocks).

↙ **Row 5 (RS):** join yarn A, inc, A x 4, turn (5 blocks).

↗ **Row 6 (WS):** inc, A x 5, fasten off yarn A, turn (6 blocks).

↙ **Row 7 (RS):** join yarn B, inc, B x 6, turn (7 blocks).

↗ **Row 8 (WS):** inc, B x 7, turn (8 blocks).

↙ **Row 9 (RS):** inc, B x 8, turn (9 blocks).

↗ **Row 10 (WS):** inc, B x 9, turn (10 blocks).

↙ **Row 11 (RS):** inc in B, NB in A, A x 9, NB in B, B x 1, turn (11 blocks).

↗ **Row 12 (WS):** inc, B x 1, A x 8, B x 2, turn (12 blocks).

↙ **Row 13 (RS):** inc, B x 1, A x 1, NB in B, B x 7, NB in A, A x 1, B x 2 changing to yarn A on last st, turn (13 blocks).

↗ **Row 14 (WS):** inc in A, B x 2, A x 1, B x 6, A x 1, B x 2, NB in A, A x 1, turn (14 blocks).

↙ **Row 15 (RS):** inc in A, B x 2, A x 1, B x 7, A x 1, B x 2, A x 1 changing to yarn B on NB when working last st, turn (15 blocks).

↗ **Row 16 (WS):** inc in B, A x 1, B x 2, A x 1, B x 1, A x 4, NB in B, B x 1, A x 1, B x 2, A x 1, B x 1, turn (16 blocks).

↙ **Row 17 (RS):** inc in B, A x 1, B x 2, A x 1, B x 2, A x 3, B x 2, A x 1, B x 2, A x 1, B x 1 changing to yarn A on NB when working last st, turn (17 blocks).

↗ **Row 18 (WS):** inc in A, B x 1, A x 1, B x 2, A x 1, B x 1, A x 4, B x 1, A x 1, B x 2, A x 1, B x 1, NB in A, A x 1, turn (18 blocks).

↙ **Row 19 (RS):** inc in A, B x 1, A x 1, B x 2, A x 1, B x 2, A x 3, B x 2, A x 1, B x 2, A x 1, B x 1, A x 1, turn (19 blocks).

Now begin decreasing at both ends.

↗ **Row 20 (WS):** dec, A x 1 and RB, B x 1, A x 1, B x 2, A x 1, B x 1, A x 4, B x 1, A x 1, B x 2, A x 1, B x 1, A x 1 and RB, turn (18 blocks).

↙ **Row 21 (RS):** dec, B x 1, A x 1, B x 2, A x 1, B x 2, A x 3, B x 2, A x 1, B x 2, A x 1, B x 1, turn (17 blocks).

↗ **Row 22 (WS):** dec, B x 1 and RB, A x 1, B x 2, A x 1, B x 1, A x 4 and RB, B x 1, A x 1, B x 2, A x 1, B x 1 and RB, turn (16 blocks).

↙ **Row 23 (RS):** dec, A x 1, B x 2, A x 1, B x 7, A x 1, B x 2, A x 1, turn (15 blocks).

↗ **Row 24 (WS):** dec, A x 1 and RB, B x 2, A x 1, B x 6, A x 1, B x 2, A x 1 and RB, turn (14 blocks).

↙ **Row 25 (RS):** dec, B x 2, A x 1, B x 7 and RB, A x 1, B x 2, turn (13 blocks).

↗ **Row 26 (WS):** dec, B x 2, A x 8, B x 2, turn (12 blocks).

↙ **Row 27 (RS):** dec, B x 1, A x 9, B x 1, turn (11 blocks).

↗ **Row 28 (WS):** dec, B x 10, turn (10 blocks).

↙ **Row 29 (RS):** dec, B x 9, turn (9 blocks).

↗ **Row 30 (WS):** dec, B x 8, turn (8 blocks).

↙ **Row 31 (RS):** dec, B x 7, fasten off yarn B, turn (7 blocks).

↗ **Row 32 (WS):** dec, A x 6, turn (6 blocks).

↙ **Row 33 (RS):** dec, A x 5, fasten off yarn A, turn (5 blocks).

↗ **Row 34 (WS):** dec, B x 4, turn (4 blocks).

↙ **Row 35 (RS):** dec, B x 3, fasten off yarn B, turn (3 blocks).

↗ **Row 36 (WS):** dec, A x 2, turn (2 blocks).

↙ **Row 37 (RS):** dec, A x 1, fasten off yarn A (1 block).

Sew in all loose ends on WS of work.

Intermittent Stripes

This striped design is bold and striking! You can work it in softer colours for a more muted look too. The blanket is worked in three sections that are joined as you go. You can also work it in one piece if you are happy with managing yarns.

SKILL LEVEL

▢ ▢ ▢

HOOK SIZE

6mm (US G-10)

BLOCK STITCH

3 tr block: (3 ch, 3 tr in ch sp)

TECHNIQUES

Join-as-you-go (see page 21)

THROW SIZE

109 x 152cm (43 x 60in)

YARN

Cascade 220® (aran/10-ply/worsted; 100g/3½oz; 200m/220yd)

- **A** 8505 White – 5 balls
- **B** 4002 Jet – 3 balls
- **C** 1058 Nimbus Cloud – 3 balls
- **D** 9668 Paprika – 3 balls

ABBREVIATIONS & STITCHES

ch	chain
ch sp	chain space
dec	sl st in next 3 sts, sl st into 3-ch sp
inc	ch 6, 1 tr in fourth ch from hook, 1 tr in next 2 ch, sl st into ch sp of next block
inc join	ch 3, sl st in next gap between 2 blocks, turn
rep	repeat
RS	right side
sl st	slip stitch
st(s)	stitch(es)
tr	treble crochet
WS	wrong side
↙ / ↗	direction of work

Throw

Section 1

- ↙ **Row 1 (RS):** using yarn A, ch 6, 1 tr in fourth ch from hook, 1 tr in next 2 ch, turn (1 block).
- ↗ **Row 2 (WS):** inc, A x 1, turn (2 blocks).
- ↙ **Row 3 (RS):** inc, A x 2 changing to yarn B when working last st, fasten off yarn A, turn (3 blocks).
- ↗ **Row 4 (WS):** inc, B x 3, turn (4 blocks).
- ↙ **Row 5 (RS):** inc, B x 4, turn (5 blocks).
- ↗ **Row 6 (WS):** inc, B x 5, turn (6 blocks).
- ↙ **Row 7 (RS):** inc, B x 6, turn (7 blocks).
- ↗ **Row 8 (WS):** inc, B x 7, turn (8 blocks).
- ↙ **Row 9 (RS):** inc, B x 8, turn (9 blocks).
- ↗ **Row 10 (WS):** inc, B x 9 changing to yarn A when working last st, fasten off yarn B, turn (10 blocks).
- ↙ **Row 11 (RS):** inc, A x 10, turn (11 blocks).
- ↗ **Row 12 (WS):** inc, A x 11, turn (12 blocks).
- ↙ **Row 13 (RS):** inc, A x 12, turn (13 blocks).
- ↗ **Row 14 (WS):** inc, A x 13 changing to yarn C when working last st, fasten off yarn A, turn (14 blocks).
- ↙ **Row 15 (RS):** inc, C x 1, B x 11, join in new skein in yarn C, C x 2, turn (15 blocks).
- ↗ **Row 16 (WS):** inc, C x 2, B x 10, C x 3, turn (16 blocks).
- ↙ **Row 17 (RS):** inc, C x 2, B x 11, C x 3, turn (17 blocks).
- ↗ **Row 18 (WS):** inc, C x 3, B x 10, C x 4, turn (18 blocks).
- ↙ **Row 19 (RS):** inc, C x 3, B x 11, C x 4, turn (19 blocks).
- ↗ **Row 20 (WS):** inc, C x 4, B x 10, C x 5, turn (20 blocks).

SECTION 1

SECTION 2

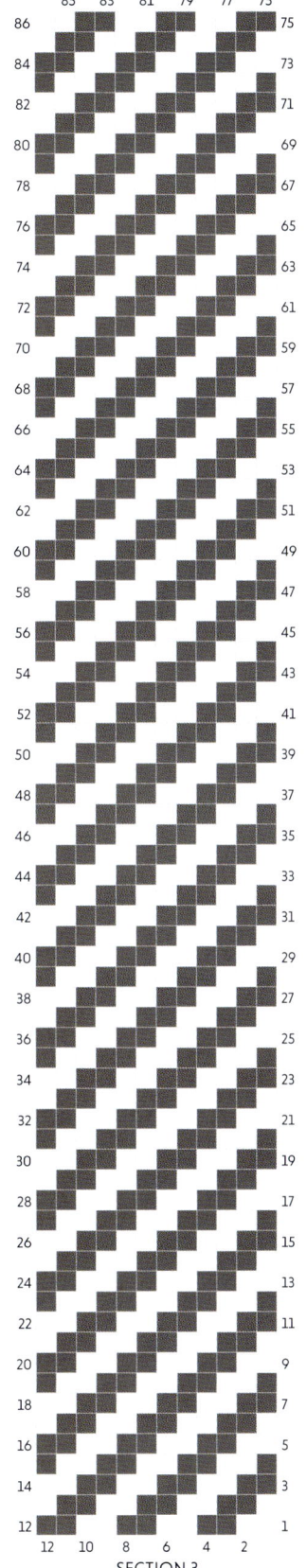

SECTION 3

↙ **Row 21 (RS):** inc, C x 4, B x 11, C x 5 changing to yarn A when working last st, fasten off yarns B and C, turn (21 blocks).

↗ **Row 22 (WS):** inc, A x 21, turn (22 blocks).

↙ **Row 23 (RS):** inc, A x 22, turn (23 blocks).

↗ **Row 24 (WS):** inc, A x 23, turn (24 blocks).

↙ **Row 25 (RS):** inc, A x 24 changing to yarn C when working last st, fasten off yarn A, turn (25 blocks).

↗ **Row 26 (WS):** inc, C x 7, B x 11, C x 7, turn (26 blocks).

↙ **Row 27 (RS):** inc, C x 7, B x 11, C x 8, turn (27 blocks).

↗ **Row 28 (WS):** inc, C x 8, B x 11, C x 8, turn (28 blocks).

↙ **Row 29 (RS):** inc, C x 8, B x 11, C x 9, turn (29 blocks).

↗ **Row 30 (WS):** inc, C x 9, B x 11, C x 9, turn (30 blocks).

↙ **Row 31 (RS):** inc, C x 9, B x 11, C x 10, turn (31 blocks).

↗ **Row 32 (WS):** inc, C x 10, B x 11, C x 10 changing to yarn A when working last st, fasten off yarns B and C, turn (32 blocks).

↙ **Row 33 (RS):** inc, A x 32, turn (33 blocks).

Corner: start decreasing on WS.

↗ **Row 34 (WS):** dec, A x 33, turn (33 blocks).

↙ **Row 35 (RS):** inc, A x 32, turn (33 blocks).

↗ **Row 36 (WS):** dec, A x 33 changing to yarn C when working last st, turn (33 blocks).

↙ **Row 37 (RS):** inc, C x 12, B x 11, C x 9, turn (33 blocks).

↗ **Row 38 (WS):** dec, C x 9, B x 11, C x 13, turn (33 blocks).

↙ **Row 39 (RS):** inc, C x 13, B x 11, C x 8, turn (33 blocks).

↗ **Row 40 (WS):** dec, C x 8, B x 11, C x 14, turn (33 blocks).

↙ **Row 41 (RS):** inc, C x 14, B x 11, C x 7, turn (33 blocks).

↗ **Row 42 (WS):** dec, C x 6, B x 11, C x 15, turn (33 blocks).

↙ **Row 43 (RS):** inc, C x 15, B x 11, C x 6, fasten off yarns B and C, turn (33 blocks).

↗ **Row 44 (WS):** join yarn A in last ch sp made, A x 33, turn (33 blocks).

↙ **Row 45 (RS):** inc, A x 32, turn (33 blocks).

↗ **Row 46 (WS):** dec, A x 33, turn (33 blocks).

↙ **Row 47 (RS):** inc, A x 32, fasten off yarn A, turn (33 blocks).

↗ **Row 48 (WS):** join yarn C in last ch sp made, C x 4, B x 11, C x 18, turn (33 blocks).

↙ **Row 49 (RS):** inc, C x 18, B x 11, C x 3, turn (33 blocks).

↗ **Row 50 (WS):** dec, C x 3, B x 11, C x 19, turn (33 blocks).

↙ **Row 51 (RS):** inc, C x 19, B x 11, C x 2, turn (33 blocks).

↗ **Row 52 (WS):** dec, C x 2, B x 11, C x 20, turn (33 blocks).

↙ **Row 53 (RS):** inc, C x 20, B x 11, C x 1, turn (33 blocks).

↗ **Row 54 (WS):** dec, C x 1, B x 11, C x 21 changing to yarn A when working last st, fasten off yarns B and C, turn (33 blocks).

↙ **Row 55 (RS):** inc, A x 32, turn (33 blocks).

↗ **Row 56 (WS):** dec, A x 33, turn (33 blocks).

↙ **Row 57 (RS):** inc, A x 32, turn (33 blocks).

↗ **Row 58 (WS):** dec, A x 32 changing to yarn C when working last st, fasten off yarn A, turn (33 blocks).

↙ **Row 59 (RS):** inc, C x 23, B x 9, turn (33 blocks).

↗ **Row 60 (WS):** dec, B x 9, C x 24, turn (33 blocks).

↙ **Row 61 (RS):** inc, C x 24, B x 8, turn (33 blocks).

LAYOUT CHART

3   2   1

↗ Row 62 (WS): dec, B x 8, C x 25, turn (33 blocks).

↙ Row 63 (RS): inc, C x 25, B x 7, turn (33 blocks).

↗ Row 64 (WS): dec, B x 7, C x 26, turn (33 blocks).

↙ Row 65 (RS): inc, C x 26, B x 6, fasten off yarns C and B, turn (33 blocks).

↗ Row 66 (WS): join yarn A in last ch sp made, A x 33, turn (33 blocks).

↙ Row 67 (RS): inc, A x 32, turn (33 blocks).

↗ Row 68 (WS): dec, A x 33, turn (33 blocks).

↙ Row 69 (RS): inc, A x 32, fasten off yarn A, turn (33 blocks).

↗ Row 70 (WS): join yarn B in last ch sp made, B x 4, C x 29, turn (33 blocks).

↙ Row 71 (RS): inc, C x 29, B x 3, turn (33 blocks).

↗ Row 72 (WS): dec, B x 3, C x 30, turn (33 blocks).

↙ Row 73 (RS): inc, C x 30, B x 2, turn (33 blocks).

↗ Row 74 (WS): dec, B x 2, C x 31, turn (33 blocks).

↙ Row 75 (RS): inc, C x 31, B x 1, turn (33 blocks).

Corner: start decreasing on RS.

↗ Row 76 (WS): dec, B x 1, C x 31, fasten off yarns B and C, turn (32 blocks).

↙ Row 77 (RS): join yarn A in last ch sp made, A x 31, turn (31 blocks).

↗ Row 78 (WS): dec, A x 30, turn (30 blocks).

↙ Row 79 (RS): dec, A x 29, turn (29 blocks).

↗ Row 80 (WS): dec, A x 28, fasten off yarn A, turn (28 blocks).

↙ Row 81 (RS): join yarn C in last ch sp made, C x 27, turn (27 blocks).

↗ Row 82 (WS): dec, C x 26, turn (26 blocks).

↙ Row 83 (RS): dec, C x 25, turn (25 blocks).

↗ Row 84 (WS): dec, C x 24, turn (24 blocks).

↙ Row 85 (RS): dec, C x 23, turn (23 blocks).

↗ Row 86 (WS): dec, C x 22, turn (22 blocks).

↙ Row 87 (RS): dec, C x 21, fasten off yarn C, turn (21 blocks).

↗ Row 88 (WS): join yarn A in last ch sp made, A x 20, turn (20 blocks).

↙ Row 89 (RS): dec, A x 19, turn (19 blocks).

↗ Row 90 (WS): dec, A x 18, turn (18 blocks).

↙ Row 91 (RS): dec, A x 17, turn (17 blocks).

↗ Row 92 (WS): join yarn C in last ch sp made, C x 16, turn (16 blocks).

↙ Row 93 (RS): dec, C x 15, turn (15 blocks).

↗ Row 94 (WS): dec, C x 14, turn (14 blocks).

↙ Row 95 (RS): dec, C x 13, turn (13 blocks).

↗ Row 96 (WS): dec, C x 12, turn (12 blocks).

↙ Row 97 (RS): dec, C x 11, turn (11 blocks).

↗ Row 98 (WS): dec, C x 10, fasten off yarn C, turn (10 blocks).

↙ Row 99 (RS): join yarn A in last ch sp made, A x 9, turn (9 blocks).

↗ Row 100 (WS): dec, A x 8, turn (8 blocks).

↙ Row 101 (RS): dec, A x 7, turn (7 blocks).

↗ Row 102 (WS): dec, A x 6, fasten off yarn A, turn (6 blocks).

↙ Row 103 (RS): join yarn C in last ch sp made, C x 5, turn (5 blocks).

↗ Row 104 (WS): dec, C x 4, turn (4 blocks).

↙ Row 105 (RS): dec, C x 3, turn (3 blocks).

↗ Row 106 (WS): dec, C x 2, turn (2 blocks).

↙ Row 107 (RS): dec, C x 1, fasten off yarn C (1 block).

Section 2

Join yarn D to bottom left-hand corner of Section 1, ch 3, sl st in gap before next block of Section 1, turn.

↙ Row 1 (RS): D x 1, turn (1 block).

↗ Row 2 (WS): inc, D x 1, inc join (2 blocks).

↙ Row 3 (RS): D x 3, turn (3 blocks).

↗ Row 4 (WS): inc, D x 3, inc join (4 blocks).

↙ Row 5 (RS): D x 5, turn (5 blocks).

↗ Row 6 (WS): inc, D x 6, inc join (6 blocks).

↙ Row 7 (RS): D x 7, turn (7 blocks).

↗ Row 8 (WS): inc, D x 8, inc join (8 blocks).

↙ Row 9 (RS): D x 9, turn (9 blocks).

↗ Row 10 (WS): inc, D x 10, inc join (10 blocks).

Corner: start decreasing on WS.

↙ Row 11 (RS): inc, D x 9, turn (10 blocks).

↗ Row 12 (WS): dec, D x 10, inc join (10 blocks).

Rep rows 11 and 12 thirty-one times in total.

↙ Row 75 (RS): D x 10, turn (10 blocks).

Corner: start decreasing on RS.

↗ Row 76 (WS): dec, D x 9, turn (9 blocks).

↙ Row 77 (RS): dec, D x 8, turn (8 blocks).

↗ Row 78 (WS): dec, D x 7, turn (7 blocks).

↙ Row 79 (RS): dec, D x 6, turn (6 blocks).

↗ Row 80 (WS): dec, D x 5, turn (5 blocks).

↙ Row 81 (RS): dec, D x 4, turn (4 blocks).

↗ Row 82 (WS): dec, D x 3, turn (3 blocks).

↙ Row 83 (RS): dec, D x 2, turn (2 blocks).

↗ Row 84 (WS): dec, D x 1, fasten off yarn D (1 block).

Section 3

Join yarn A to bottom left-hand corner of Section 2 with RS facing, ch 3, sl st into gap before next block of Section 2, turn.

↙ Row 1 (RS): A x 1, turn (1 block).

↗ Row 2 (WS): inc, A x 1, changing to yarn B

when working last st, fasten off yarn A, inc join (2 blocks).

↙ Row 3 (RS): B x 3, turn (3 blocks).

↗ Row 4 (WS): inc, B x 3 changing to yarn A when working last st, inc join (4 blocks).

↙ Row 5 (RS): A x 5, turn (5 blocks).

↗ Row 6 (WS): inc, A x 5 changing to yarn B when working last st, inc join (6 blocks).

↙ Row 7 (RS): B x 7, turn (7 blocks).

↗ Row 8 (WS): inc, B x 7 changing to yarn A when working last st, inc join (8 blocks).

↙ Row 9 (RS): A x 9, turn (9 blocks).

↗ Row 10 (WS): inc, A x 10 changing to yarn B when working last st, inc join (10 blocks).

↙ Row 11 (RS): B x 11, turn (11 blocks).

↗ Row 12 (WS): inc, B x 11 changing to yarn A when working last st, inc join (12 blocks).

Corner: start decreasing on WS.

↙ Row 13 (RS): A x 12, turn (12 blocks).

↗ Row 14 (WS): dec, A x 12 changing to yarn B when working last st, inc join (12 blocks).

↙ Row 15 (RS): B x 12, turn (12 blocks).

↗ Row 16 (WS): dec, B x 12 changing to yarn A when working last st, inc join (12 blocks).

Rep rows 13–16 fourteen times in total.

↙ Row 73 (RS): A x 12, turn (12 blocks).

↗ Row 74 (WS): dec, A x 12 changing to yarn B when working last st, fasten off yarn A, turn (12 blocks).

↙ Row 75 (RS): B x 12, turn (12 blocks).

Corner: start decreasing on RS.

↗ Row 76 (WS): dec, B x 11, fasten off yarn B, turn (11 blocks).

↙ Row 77 (RS): join yarn A in last ch sp made, A x 10, turn (10 blocks).

↗ Row 78 (WS): dec, A x 9, fasten off yarn A, turn (9 blocks).

↙ Row 79 (RS): join yarn B in last ch sp made, B x 8, turn (8 blocks).

↗ Row 80 (WS): dec, B x 7, fasten off yarn B, turn (7 blocks).

↙ Row 81 (RS): join yarn A in last ch sp made, A x 6, turn (6 blocks).

↗ Row 82 (WS): dec, A x 5, fasten off yarn A, turn (5 blocks).

↙ Row 83 (RS): join yarn B in last ch sp made, B x 4, turn (4 blocks).

↗ Row 84 (WS): dec, B x 3, fasten off yarn B, turn (3 blocks).

↙ Row 85 (RS): join yarn A in last ch sp made, A x 2, turn (2 blocks).

↗ Row 86 (WS): dec, A x 1, fasten off yarn A (1 block).

Sew in all loose ends on WS of work.

Gingham

This lovely checkered pattern can be worked in any colourway you choose. Alternatively, you could use random colours to work each section for a patchwork throw.

SKILL LEVEL

☐ ☐ ☐

HOOK SIZE

6mm (US G-10)

BLOCK STITCH

3 tr block: (3 ch, 3 tr in ch sp)

THROW SIZE

109 x 152cm (43 x 60in)

YARN

Cascade 220® (aran/10-ply/worsted; 100g/3½oz; 200m/220yd)

 A 9469 Hot Pink – 4 balls

 B 9478 Cotton Candy – 6 balls

 C 8505 White – 3 balls

ABBREVIATIONS & STITCHES

ch sp chain space

dec sl st in next 3 sts, sl st into 3-ch sp

inc ch 6, 1 tr in fourth ch from hook, 1 tr in next 2 ch, sl st into ch sp of next block

RS right side

sl st slip stitch

st(s) stitch(es)

tr treble crochet

WS wrong side

↙ / ↗ direction of work

Throw

↙ **Row 1 (RS):** using yarn A, ch 6, 1 tr in third ch from hook and next 2 ch, turn (1 block).

↗ **Row 2 (WS):** inc, A x 1, turn (2 blocks).

↙ **Row 3 (RS):** inc, A x 2, turn (3 blocks).

↗ **Row 4 (WS):** inc, A x 3, turn (4 blocks).

↙ **Row 5 (RS):** inc, A x 4, changing to yarn B when working last st, turn (5 blocks).

↗ **Row 6 (WS):** inc in B, A x 4, B x 1, turn (6 blocks).

↙ **Row 7 (RS):** inc, B x 1, A x 3, B x 2, turn (7 blocks).

↗ **Row 8 (WS):** inc, B x 2, A x 2, B x 3, turn (8 blocks).

↙ **Row 9 (RS):** inc, B x 3, A x 1, B x 4, fasten off yarn A, turn (9 blocks).

↗ **Row 10 (WS):** inc, B x 9, changing to yarn A when working last st, turn (10 blocks).

↙ **Row 11 (RS):** inc in A, B x 4, C x 1, B x 4, A x 1, turn (11 blocks).

↗ **Row 12 (WS):** inc, A x 1, B x 3, C x 2, B x 3, A x 2, turn (12 blocks).

↙ **Row 13 (RS):** inc, A x 2, B x 2, C x 3, B x 2, A x 3, turn (13 blocks).

↗ **Row 14 (WS):** inc, A x 3, B x 1, fasten off yarn B, C x 4, B x 1, A x 4, turn (14 blocks).

↙ **Row 15 (RS):** inc, A x 4, C x 5, A x 5, changing to yarn B when working last st, turn (15 blocks).

↗ **Row 16 (WS):** inc in B, A x 4, B x 1, C x 4, B x 1, A x 4, B x 1, turn (16 blocks).

↙ **Row 17 (RS):** inc, B x 1, A x 3, B x 2, C x 3, B x 2, A x 3, B x 2, turn (17 blocks).

↗ **Row 18 (WS):** inc, B x 2, A x 2, B x 3, C x 2, B x 3, A x 2, B x 3, turn (18 blocks).

↙ **Row 19 (RS):** inc, B x 3, A x 1, fasten off yarn

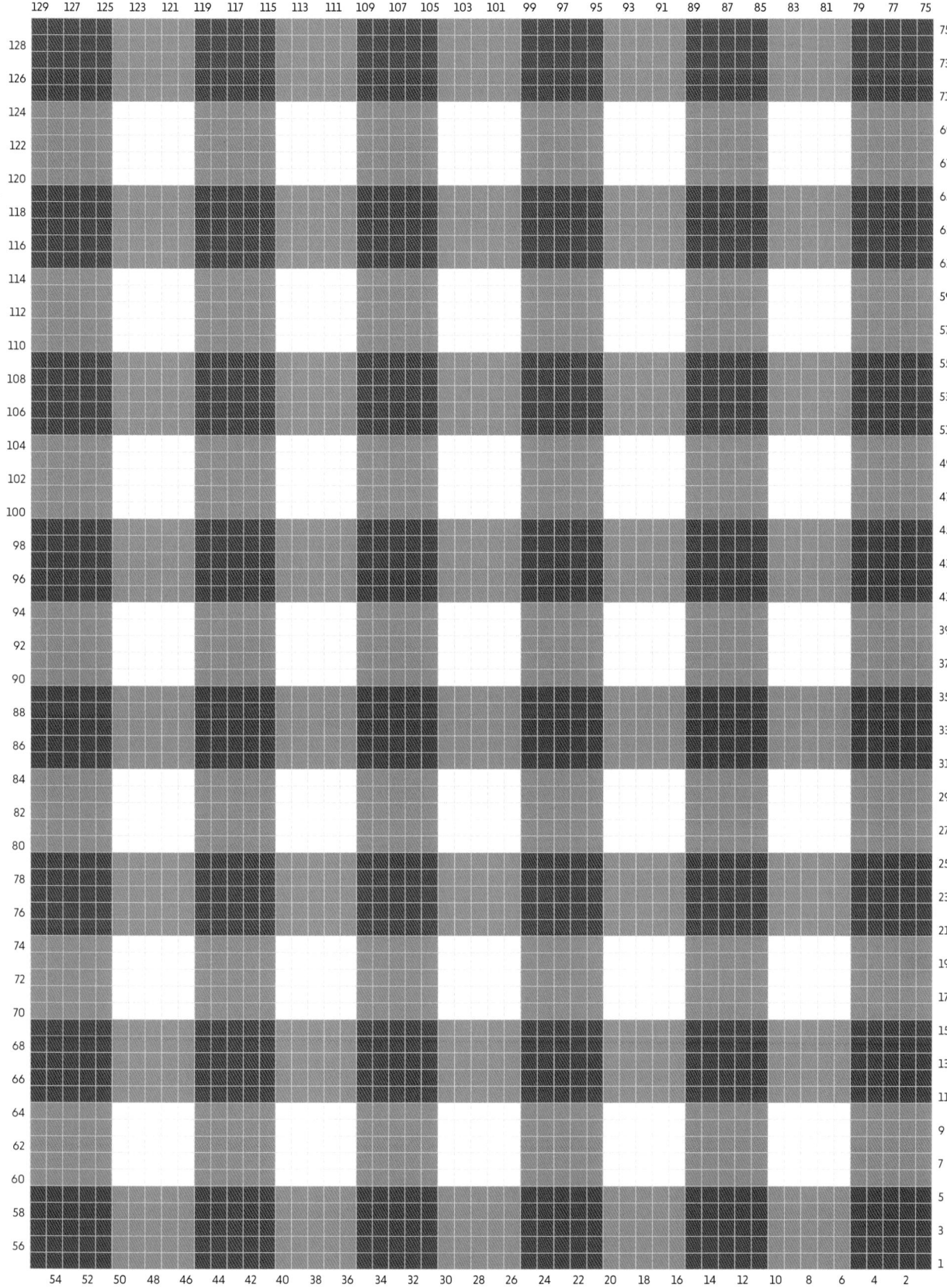

A, B x 4, C x 1, fasten off yarn C, B x 4, A x 1, fasten off yarn A, B x 4, turn (19 blocks).

↗ Row 20 (WS): inc, B x 19, changing to yarn A when working last st, turn (20 blocks).

↙ Row 21 (RS): inc in A, B x 4, C x 1, B x 4, A x 1, B x 4, C x 1, B x 4, A x 1, turn (21 blocks).

↗ Row 22 (WS): inc, A x 1, B x 3, C x 2, B x 3, A x 2, B x 3, C x 2, B x 3, A x 2, turn (22 blocks).

↙ Row 23 (RS): inc, A x 2, B x 2, C x 3, B x 2, A x 3, B x 2, C x 3, B x 2, A x 3, turn (23 blocks).

↗ Row 24 (WS): inc, A x 3, B x 1, fasten off yarn B, C x 4, B x 1, A x 4, B x 1, C x 4, B x 1, A x 4, turn (24 blocks).

↙ Row 25 (RS): inc, A x 4, C x 5, A x 5, C x 5, A x 5, changing to yarn B when working last st, turn (25 blocks).

↗ Row 26 (WS): inc in B, A x 4, B x 1, C x 4, B x 1, A x 4, B x 1, C x 4, B x 1, A x 4, B x 1, turn (26 blocks).

↙ Row 27 (RS): inc, B x 1, A x 3, B x 2, C x 3, B x 2, A x 3, B x 2, C x 3, B x 2, A x 3, B x 2, turn (27 blocks).

↗ Row 28 (WS): inc, B x 2, A x 2, B x 3, C x 2, B x 3, A x 2, B x 3, C x 2, B x 3, A x 2, B x 3, turn (28 blocks).

↙ Row 29 (RS): inc, B x 3, A x 1, fasten off yarn A, B x 4, C x 1, fasten off yarn C, B x 4, A x 1, fasten off yarn A, B x 4, C x 1, fasten off yarn C, B x 4, A x 1, fasten off yarn A, B x 4, turn (29 blocks).

↗ Row 30 (WS): inc, B x 29, changing to yarn A when working last st, turn (30 blocks).

↙ Row 31 (RS): inc in A, B x 4, C x 1, B x 4, A x 1, B x 4, C x 1, B x 4, A x 1, B x 4, C x 1, B x 4, A x 1, turn (31 blocks).

↗ Row 32 (WS): inc, A x 1, B x 3, C x 2, B x 3, A x 2, B x 3, C x 2, B x 3, A x 2, B x 3, C x 2, B x 3, A x 2, turn (32 blocks).

↙ Row 33 (RS): inc, A x 2, B x 2, C x 3, B x 2, A x 3, B x 2, C x 3, B x 2, A x 3, B x 2, C x 3, B x 2, A x 3, turn (33 blocks).

↗ Row 34 (WS): inc, A x 3, B x 1, fasten off yarn B, C x 4, B x 1, A x 4, B x 1, C x 4, B x 1, A x 4, B x 1, C x 4, B x 1, A x 4, turn (34 blocks).

↙ Row 35 (RS): inc, A x 4, C x 5, A x 5, C x 5, A x 5, C x 5, A x 5, changing to yarn B when working last st, turn (35 blocks).

↗ Row 36 (WS): inc in B, A x 4, B x 1, C x 4, B x 1, A x 4, B x 1, C x 4, B x 1, A x 4, B x 1, C x 4, B x 1, A x 4, B x 1, turn (36 blocks).

↙ Row 37 (RS): inc, B x 1, A x 3, B x 2, C x 3, B x 2, A x 3, B x 2, C x 3, B x 2, A x 3, B x 2, C x 3, B x 2, A x 3, B x 2, turn (37 blocks).

↙ Row 38 (WS): inc, B x 2, A x 2, B x 3, C x 2, B x 3, A x 2, B x 3, C x 2, B x 3, A x 2, B x 3, C x 2, B x 3, A x 2, B x 3, turn (38 blocks).

↙ Row 39 (RS): inc, B x 3, A x 1, fasten off yarn A, B x 4, C x 1, fasten off yarn C, B x 4, A x 1, fasten off yarn A, B x 4, C x 1, fasten off yarn C, B x 4, A x 1, fasten off yarn A, B x 4, C x 1, fasten off yarn C, B x 4, A x 1, fasten off yarn A, B x 4, turn (39 blocks).

↗ Row 40 (WS): inc, B x 39, changing to yarn A when working last st, turn (40 blocks).

↙ Row 41 (RS): inc in A, B x 4, C x 1, B x 4, A x 1, B x 4, C x 1, B x 4, A x 1, B x 4, C x 1, B x 4, A x 1, B x 4, C x 1, B x 4, A x 1, turn (41 blocks).

↗ Row 42 (WS): inc, A x 1, B x 3, C x 2, B x 3, A x 2, B x 3, C x 2, B x 3, A x 2, B x 3, C x 2, B x 3, A x 2, B x 3, C x 2, B x 3, A x 2, turn (42 blocks).

↙ Row 43 (RS): inc, A x 2, B x 2, C x 3, B x 2, A x 3, B x 2, C x 3, B x 2, A x 3, B x 2, C x 3, B x 2, A x 3, B x 2, C x 3, B x 2, A x 3, turn (43 blocks).

↗ Row 44 (WS): inc, A x 3, B x 1, fasten off yarn B, C x 4, B x 1, A x 4, B x 1, C x 4, B x 1, A x 4, B x 1, C x 4, B x 1, A x 4, B x 1, C x 4, B x 1, A x 4, turn (44 blocks).

↙ Row 45 (RS): inc, A x 4, C x 5, A x 5, C x 5, A x 5, C x 5, A x 5, C x 5, A x 5, changing to yarn B when working last st, turn (45 blocks).

↗ Row 46 (WS): inc in B, A x 4, B x 1, C x 4, B x 1, A x 4, B x 1, C x 4, B x 1, A x 4, B x 1, C x 4, B x 1, A x 4, B x 1, C x 4, B x 1, A x 4, B x 1, turn (46 blocks).

↙ Row 47 (RS): inc, B x 1, A x 3, B x 2, C x 3, B x 2, A x 3, B x 2, C x 3, B x 2, A x 3, B x 2, C x 3, B x 2, A x 3, B x 2, C x 3, B x 2, A x 3, B x 2, turn (47 blocks).

↗ Row 48 (WS): inc, B x 2, A x 2, B x 3, C x 2, B x 3, A x 2, B x 3, C x 2, B x 3, A x 2, B x 3, C x 2, B x 3, A x 2, B x 3, C x 2, B x 3, A x 2, B x 3, turn (48 blocks).

↙ Row 49 (RS): inc, B x 3, A x 1, fasten off yarn A, B x 4, C x 1, fasten off yarn C, B x 4, A x 1, fasten off yarn A, B x 4, C x 1, fasten off yarn C, B x 4, A x 1, fasten off yarn A, B x 4, C x 1, fasten off yarn C, B x 4, A x 1, fasten off yarn A, B x 4, C x 1, fasten off yarn C, B x 4, A x 1, fasten off yarn A, B x 4, turn (49 blocks).

↗ Row 50 (WS): inc, B x 49, changing to yarn A when working last st, turn (50 blocks).

↙ Row 51 (RS): inc in A, B x 4, C x 1, B x 4, A x 1, B x 4, C x 1, B x 4, A x 1, B x 4, C x 1, B x 4, A x 1, B x 4, C x 1, B x 4, A x 1, B x 4, C x 1, B x 4, A x 1, turn (51 blocks).

↗ Row 52 (WS): inc, A x 1, B x 3, C x 2, B x 3, A x 2, B x 3, C x 2, B x 3, A x 2, B x 3, C x 2, B x 3, A x 2, B x 3, C x 2, B x 3, A x 2, B x 3, C x 2, B x 3, A x 2, turn (52 blocks).

↙ Row 53 (RS): inc, A x 2, B x 2, C x 3, B x 2, A x 3, B x 2, C x 3, B x 2, A x 3, B x 2, C x 3, B x 2, A x 3, B x 2, C x 3, B x 2, A x 3, B x 2, C x 3, B x 2, A x 3, turn (53 blocks).

↗ Row 54 (WS): inc, A x 3, B x 1, fasten off yarn B, C x 4, B x 1, A x 4, B x 1, C x 4, B x 1, A x 4, B x 1, C x 4, B x 1, A x 4, B x 1, C x 4, B x 1, A x 4, B x 1, C x 4, B x 1, A x 4, turn (54 blocks).

↙ Row 55 (RS): inc, A x 4, C x 5, A x 5, C x 5, A x 5, C x 5, A x 5, C x 5, A x 5, C x 5, A x 5, turn (55 blocks).

Corner: start decreasing on WS.

↗ Row 56 (WS): dec, A x 4, B x 1, C x 4, B x 1, A x 4, B x 1, C x 4, B x 1, A x 4, B x 1, C x 4, B x 1, A x 4, B x 1, C x 4, B x 1, A x 4, B x 1, C x 4, B x 1, A x 4, B x 1, turn (55 blocks).

↙ Row 57 (RS): inc, B x 1, A x 3, B x 2, C x 3, B x 2, A x 3, B x 2, C x 3, B x 2, A x 3, B x 2, C x 3, B x 2, A x 3, B x 2, C x 3, B x 2, A x 3, B x 2, C x 3, B x 2, A x 3, B x 2, C x 3, B x 2, A x 3, B x 2, turn (55 blocks).

↗ Row 58 (WS): dec, A x 2, B x 3, C x 2, B x 3, A x 2, B x 3, C x 2, B x 3, A x 2, B x 3, C x 2, B x 3, A x 2, B x 3, C x 2, B x 3, A x 2, B x 3, C x 2, B x 3, A x 2, B x 3, turn (55 blocks).

↙ Row 59 (RS): inc, B x 3, A x 1, fasten off yarn A, B x 4, C x 1, fasten off yarn C, B x 4, A x 1, fasten off yarn A, B x 4, C x 1, fasten off yarn C, B x 4, A x 1, fasten off yarn A, B x 4, C x 1, fasten off yarn C, B x 4, A x 1, fasten off yarn A, B x 4, C x 1, fasten off yarn C, B x 4, A x 1, fasten off yarn A, turn (55 blocks).

↗ Row 60 (WS): dec, B x 55, changing to yarn

A when working last st, turn (55 blocks).

↙ Row 61 (RS): inc in A, B x 4, C x 1, B x 4, A x 1, B x 4, C x 1, B x 4, A x 1, B x 4, C x 1, B x 4, A x 1, B x 4, C x 1, B x 4, A x 1, B x 4, C x 1, B x 4, A x 1, B x 4, turn (55 blocks).

↗ Row 62 (WS): dec, B x 3, A x 2, B x 3, C x 2, B x 3, A x 2, B x 3, C x 2, B x 3, A x 2, B x 3, C x 2, B x 3, A x 2, B x 3, C x 2, B x 3, A x 2, B x 3, C x 2, B x 3, A x 2, turn (55 blocks).

↙ Row 63 (RS): inc, A x 2, B x 2, C x 3, B x 2, A x 3, B x 2, C x 3, B x 2, A x 3, B x 2, C x 3, B x 2, A x 3, B x 2, C x 3, B x 2, A x 3, B x 2, turn (55 blocks).

↗ Row 64 (WS): dec, B x 1, fasten off yarn B, A x 4, B x 1, C x 4, B x 1, A x 4, B x 1, C x 4, B x 1, A x 4, B x 1, fasten off yarn B, C x 4, B x 1, A x 4, B x 1, C x 4, B x 1, A x 4, B x 1, C x 4, B x 1, A x 4, turn (55 blocks).

↙ Row 65 (RS): inc, A x 4, C x 5, A x 5, C x 5, A x 5, C x 5, A x 5, C x 5, A x 5, C x 5, A x 5, turn (55 blocks).

↗ Row 66 (WS): dec, A x 4, B x 1, C x 4, B x 1, A x 4, B x 1, C x 4, B x 1, A x 4, B x 1, C x 4, B x 1, A x 4, B x 1, C x 4, B x 1, A x 4, B x 1, C x 4, B x 1, A x 4, B x 1, turn (55 blocks).

↙ Row 67 (RS): inc, B x 1, A x 3, B x 2, C x 3, B x 2, A x 3, B x 2, C x 3, B x 2, A x 3, B x 2, C x 3, B x 2, A x 3, B x 2, C x 3, B x 2, A x 3, B x 2, C x 3, B x 2, A x 3, turn (55 blocks).

↗ Row 68 (WS): dec, A x 2, B x 3, C x 2, B x 3, A x 2, B x 3, C x 2, B x 3, A x 2, B x 3, C x 2, B x 3, A x 2, B x 3, C x 2, B x 3, A x 2, B x 3, turn (55 blocks).

↙ Row 69 (RS): inc, B x 3, A x 1, fasten off yarn A, B x 4, C x 1, fasten off yarn C, B x 4, A x 1, fasten off yarn A, B x 4, C x 1, fasten off yarn C, B x 4, A x 1, fasten off yarn A, B x 4, C x 1, fasten off yarn C, B x 4, A x 1, fasten off yarn A, B x 4, C x 1, fasten off yarn C, B x 4, A x 1, fasten off yarn A, B x 4, C x 1, fasten off yarn C, B x 4, A x 1, fasten off yarn A, turn (55 blocks).

↗ Row 70 (WS): dec, B x 55, changing to yarn A when working last st, turn (55 blocks).

↙ Row 71 (RS): inc in A, B x 4, C x 1, B x 4, A x 1, B x 4, C x 1, B x 4, A x 1, B x 4, C x 1, B x 4, A x 1, B x 4, C x 1, B x 4, A x 1, B x 4, C x 1, B x 4, A x 1, B x 4, turn (55 blocks).

↗ Row 72 (WS): dec, B x 3, A x 2, B x 3, C x 2, B x 3, A x 2, B x 3, C x 2, B x 3, A x 2, B x 3, C x 2, B x 3, A x 2,

B x 3, C x 2, B x 3, A x 2, turn (55 blocks).

↙ Row 73 (RS): inc, A x 2, B x 2, C x 3, B x 2, A x 3, B x 2, C x 3, B x 2, A x 3, B x 2, C x 3, B x 2, A x 3, B x 2, C x 3, B x 2, A x 3, B x 2, C x 3, B x 2, A x 3, B x 2, turn (55 blocks).

↗ Row 74 (WS): dec, B x 1, fasten off yarn B, A x 4, B x 1, C x 4, B x 1, A x 4, B x 1, C x 4, B x 1, A x 4, B x 1, C x 4, B x 1, A x 4, B x 1, C x 4, B x 1, A x 4, B x 1, C x 4, B x 1, A x 4, turn (55 blocks).

↙ Row 75 (RS): inc, A x 4, C x 5, A x 5, C x 5, A x 5, C x 5, A x 5, C x 5, A x 5, C x 5, A x 5, turn (55 blocks).

Corner: start decreasing on RS.

↗ Row 76 (WS): dec, A x 4, B x 1, C x 4, B x 1, A x 4, B x 1, C x 4, B x 1, A x 4, B x 1, C x 4, B x 1, A x 4, B x 1, C x 4, B x 1, A x 4, B x 1, C x 4, B x 1, A x 4, turn (54 blocks).

↙ Row 77 (RS): dec, A x 3, B x 2, C x 3, B x 2, A x 3, B x 2, C x 3, B x 2, A x 3, B x 2, C x 3, B x 2, A x 3, B x 2, C x 3, B x 2, A x 3, B x 2, C x 3, B x 2, A x 3, turn (53 blocks).

↗ Row 78 (WS): dec, A x 2, B x 3, C x 2, B x 3, A x 2, B x 3, C x 2, B x 3, A x 2, B x 3, C x 2, B x 3, A x 2, B x 3, C x 2, B x 3, A x 2, B x 3, C x 2, B x 3, A x 2, turn (52 blocks).

↙ Row 79 (RS): dec, A x 1, fasten off yarn A, B x 4, C x 1, fasten off yarn C, B x 4, A x 1, fasten off yarn A, B x 4, C x 1, fasten off yarn C, B x 4, A x 1, fasten off yarn A, B x 4, C x 1, fasten off yarn C, B x 4, A x 1, fasten off yarn A, B x 4, C x 1, fasten off yarn C, B x 4, A x 1, fasten off yarn A, B x 4, C x 1, fasten off yarn C, B x 4, A x 1, fasten off yarn A, turn (51 blocks).

↗ Row 80 (WS): dec, B x 50, turn (50 blocks).

↙ Row 81 (RS): dec, B x 4, A x 1, B x 4, C x 1, B x 4, A x 1, B x 4, C x 1, B x 4, A x 1, B x 4, C x 1, B x 4, A x 1, B x 4, C x 1, B x 4, A x 1, B x 4, turn (49 blocks).

↗ Row 82 (WS): dec, B x 3, A x 2, B x 3, C x 2, B x 3, A x 2, B x 3, C x 2, B x 3, A x 2, B x 3, C x 2, B x 3, A x 2, B x 3, C x 2, B x 3, A x 2, B x 3, turn (48 blocks).

↙ Row 83 (RS): dec, B x 2, A x 3, B x 2, C x 3, B x 2, A x 3, B x 2, C x 3, B x 2, A x 3, B x 2, C x 3, B x 2, A x 3, B x 2, C x 3, B x 2, A x 3, B x 2, turn (47 blocks).

↗ Row 84 (WS): dec, B x 1, fasten off yarn B, A x 4, B x 1, C x 4, B x 1, A x 4, B x 1, C x 4, B x 1, A x 4, B x 1,

C x 4, B x 1, A x 4, B x 1, turn (46 blocks).

↙ Row 85 (RS): dec, A x 5, C x 5, A x 5, C x 5, A x 5, C x 5, A x 5, C x 5, A x 5, turn (45 blocks).

↗ Row 86 (WS): dec, A x 4, B x 1, C x 4, B x 1, A x 4, B x 1, C x 4, B x 1, A x 4, B x 1, C x 4, B x 1, A x 4, B x 1, C x 4, B x 1, A x 4, turn (44 blocks).

↙ Row 87 (RS): dec, A x 3, B x 2, C x 3, B x 2, A x 3, B x 2, C x 3, B x 2, A x 3, B x 2, C x 3, B x 2, A x 3, B x 2, C x 3, B x 2, A x 3, turn (43 blocks).

↗ Row 88 (WS): dec, A x 2, B x 3, C x 2, B x 3, A x 2, B x 3, C x 2, B x 3, A x 2, B x 3, C x 2, B x 3, A x 2, B x 3, C x 2, B x 3, A x 2, turn (42 blocks).

↙ Row 89 (RS): dec, A x 1, fasten off yarn A, B x 4, C x 1, fasten off yarn C, B x 4, A x 1, fasten off yarn A, B x 4, C x 1, fasten off yarn C, B x 4, A x 1, fasten off yarn A, B x 4, C x 1, fasten off yarn C, B x 4, A x 1, fasten off yarn A, B x 4, C x 1, fasten off yarn C, B x 4, A x 1, fasten off yarn A, turn (41 blocks).

↗ Row 90 (WS): dec, B x 40, turn (40 blocks).

↙ Row 91 (RS): dec, B x 4, A x 1, B x 4, C x 1, B x 4, A x 1, B x 4, C x 1, B x 4, A x 1, B x 4, C x 1, B x 4, A x 1, B x 4, turn (39 blocks).

↗ Row 92 (WS): dec, B x 3, A x 2, B x 3, C x 2, B x 3, A x 2, B x 3, C x 2, B x 3, A x 2, B x 3, C x 2, B x 3, A x 2, B x 3, turn (38 blocks).

↙ Row 93 (RS): dec, B x 2, A x 3, B x 2, C x 3, B x 2, A x 3, B x 2, C x 3, B x 2, A x 3, B x 2, C x 3, B x 2, A x 3, B x 2, turn (37 blocks).

↗ Row 94 (WS): dec, B x 1, fasten off yarn B, A x 4, B x 1, fasten off yarn B, C x 4, B x 1, fasten off yarn B, A x 4, B x 1, fasten off yarn B, C x 4, B x 1, fasten off yarn B, A x 4, B x 1, fasten off yarn B, C x 4, B x 1, fasten off yarn B, A x 4, B x 1, fasten off yarn B, turn (36 blocks).

↙ Row 95 (RS): dec, A x 5, C x 5, A x 5, C x 5, A x 5, C x 5, A x 5, turn (35 blocks).

↗ Row 96 (WS): dec, A x 4, B x 1, C x 4, B x 1, A x 4, B x 1, C x 4, B x 1, A x 4, B x 1, C x 4, B x 1, A x 4, turn (34 blocks).

↙ Row 97 (RS): dec, A x 3, B x 2, C x 3, B x 2, A x 3, B x 2, C x 3, B x 2, A x 3, B x 2, C x 3, B x 2, A x 3, turn (33 blocks).

↗ Row 98 (WS): dec, A x 2, B x 3, C x 2, B x 3, A x 2, B x 3, C x 2, B x 3, A x 2, B x 3, C x 2,

B x 3, A x 2, turn (32 blocks).

↙ Row 99 (RS): dec, A x 1, fasten off yarn A, B x 4, C x 1, fasten off yarn C, B x 4, A x 1, fasten off yarn A, B x 4, C x 1, fasten off yarn C, B x 4, A x 1, fasten off yarn A, B x 4, C x 1, fasten off yarn C, B x 4, A x 1, fasten off yarn A, turn (31 blocks).

↗ Row 100 (WS): dec, B x 30, turn (30 blocks).

↙ Row 101 (RS): dec, B x 4, A x 1, B x 4, C x 1, B x 4, A x 1, B x 4, C x 1, B x 4, A x 1, B x 4, turn (29 blocks).

↗ Row 102 (WS): dec, B x 3, A x 2, B x 3, C x 2, B x 3, A x 2, B x 3, C x 2, B x 3, A x 2, B x 3, turn (28 blocks).

↙ Row 103 (RS): dec, B x 2, A x 3, B x 2, C x 3, B x 2, A x 3, B x 2, C x 3, B x 2, A x 3, B x 2, turn (27 blocks).

↗ Row 104 (WS): dec, B x 1, fasten off yarn B, A x 4, B x 1, C x 4, B x 1, A x 4, B x 1, C x 4, B x 1, A x 4, B x 1, turn (26 blocks).

↙ Row 105 (RS): dec, A x 5, C x 5, A x 5, C x 5, A x 5, turn (25 blocks).

↗ Row 106 (WS): dec, A x 4, B x 1, C x 4, B x 1, A x 4, B x 1, C x 4, B x 1, A x 4, turn (24 blocks).

↙ Row 107 (RS): dec, A x 3, B x 2, C x 3, B x 2, A x 3, B x 2, C x 3, B x 2, A x 3, turn (23 blocks).

↗ Row 108 (WS): dec, A x 2, B x 3, C x 2, B x 3, A x 2, B x 3, C x 2, B x 3, A x 2, turn (22 blocks).

↙ Row 109 (RS): dec, A x 1, fasten off yarn A, B x 4, C x 1, fasten off yarn C, B x 4, A x 1, fasten off yarn A, B x 4, C x 1, fasten off yarn C, B x 4, A x 1, fasten off yarn A, turn (21 blocks).

↗ Row 110 (WS): dec, B x 20, turn (20 blocks).

↙ Row 111 (RS): dec, B x 4, A x 1, B x 4, C x 1, B x 4, A x 1, B x 4, turn (19 blocks).

↗ Row 112 (WS): dec, B x 3, A x 2, B x 3, C x 2, B x 3, A x 2, B x 3, turn (18 blocks).

↙ Row 113 (RS): dec, B x 2, A x 3, B x 2, C x 3, B x 2, A x 3, B x 2, turn (17 blocks).

↗ Row 114 (WS): dec, B x 1, fasten off yarn B, A x 4, B x 1, C x 4, B x 1, A x 4, B x 1, turn (16 blocks).

↙ Row 115 (RS): dec, A x 5, C x 5, A x 5, turn (15 blocks).

↗ Row 116 (WS): dec, A x 4, B x 1, C x 4, B x 1, A x 4, turn (14 blocks).

↙ Row 117 (RS): dec, A x 3, B x 2, C x 3, B x 2, A x 3, turn (13 blocks).

↗ Row 118 (WS): dec, A x 2, B x 3, C x 2, B x 3, A x 2, turn (12 blocks).

↙ Row 119 (RS): dec, A x 1, fasten off yarn A, B x 4, C x 1, fasten off yarn C, B x 4, A x 1, fasten off yarn A, turn (11 blocks).

↗ Row 120 (WS): dec, B x 10, turn (10 blocks).

↙ Row 121 (RS): dec, B x 4, A x 1, B x 4, turn (9 blocks).

↗ Row 122 (WS): dec, B x 3, A x 2, B x 3, turn (8 blocks).

↙ Row 123 (RS): dec, B x 2, A x 3, B x 2, turn (7 blocks).

↗ Row 124 (WS): dec, B x 1, fasten off yarn B, A x 4, B x 1, fasten off yarn B, turn (6 blocks).

↙ Row 125 (RS): dec, A x 5, turn (5 blocks).

↗ Row 126 (WS): dec, A x 4, turn (4 blocks).

↙ Row 127 (RS): dec, A x 3, turn (3 blocks).

↗ Row 128 (WS): dec, A x 2, turn (2 blocks).

↙ Row 129 (RS): dec, A x 1, fasten off yarn A (1 block).

Sew in all loose ends on WS of work.

chapter 3
PROJECTS

Chunky Rug

This simple rug, using just two shades of grey, is given a bit of punch with tassels in a contrasting colour. Using a super-chunky-weight yarn means this project works up really quickly and feels divine under your feet!

SKILL LEVEL

■ □ □

HOOK SIZE

11.5mm (US P-16)

BLOCK STITCH

3 tr block: (3 ch, 3 tr in ch sp)

THROW SIZE

75 x 130cm (30 x 51in)
without the tassels

YARN

Cascade Magnum (super chunky/super bulky; 250g/8⅞oz; 113m/124yd)

	A	9549 Koala Bear – 3 balls
	B	8400 Charcoal – 3 balls
	C	0086 Golden Kiwi – 1 ball

ABBREVIATIONS & STITCHES

ch	chain
ch sp	chain space
dec	sl st in next 3 sts, sl st into 3-ch sp
inc	ch 6, 1 tr in fourth ch from hook, 1 tr in next 2 ch, sl st into ch sp of next block
RS	right side
sl st	slip stitch
st(s)	stitch(es)
tr	treble crochet
WS	wrong side
↙/↗	direction of work

Rug

↙ Row 1 (RS): using yarn A, 6 ch, 1 tr in fourth ch from hook, 1 tr in next 2 ch, turn (1 block).

↗ Row 2 (WS): inc, A x 1, turn (2 blocks).

↙ Row 3 (RS): inc, A x 2, turn (3 blocks).

↗ Row 4 (WS): inc, A x 3, fasten off yarn A, turn (4 blocks).

↙ Row 5 (RS): join yarn B in last st made, inc, B x 4, turn (5 blocks).

↗ Row 6 (WS): inc, B x 5, turn (6 blocks).

↙ Row 7 (RS): inc, B x 6, turn (7 blocks).

↗ Row 8 (WS): inc, B x 7, fasten off yarn B, turn (8 blocks).

↙ Row 9 (RS): join yarn A in last st made, inc, A x 8, turn (9 blocks).

↗ Row 10 (WS): inc, A x 9, turn (10 blocks).

↙ Row 11 (RS): inc, A x 10, turn (11 blocks).

↗ Row 12 (WS): inc, A x 11, fasten off yarn A, turn (12 blocks).

↙ Row 13 (RS): join yarn B in last st made, inc, B x 12, turn (13 blocks).

↗ Row 14 (WS): inc, B x 13, turn (14 blocks).

↙ Row 15 (RS): inc, B x 14, turn (15 blocks).

↗ Row 16 (WS): inc, B x 15, turn (16 blocks).

Corner: start decreasing on RS.

↙ Row 17 (RS): join yarn A in last ch sp made, A x 16, turn (16 blocks).

↗ Row 18 (WS): inc, A x 16, turn (16 blocks).

↙ Row 19 (RS): dec, A x 16, turn (16 blocks).

↗ Row 20 (WS): inc, A x 16, fasten off yarn A, turn (16 blocks).

↙ Row 21 (RS): join yarn B in last ch sp made, B x 16, turn (16 blocks).

↗ Row 22 (WS): inc, B x 16, turn (16 blocks).

↙ Row 23 (RS): dec, B x 16, turn (16 blocks).

↗ Row 24 (WS): inc, B x 16, fasten off yarn B, turn (16 blocks).

↙ Row 25 (RS): join yarn A in last ch sp made, A x 16, turn (16 blocks).

↗ Row 26 (WS): inc, A x 16, turn (16 blocks).

↙ Row 27 (RS): dec, A x 16, turn (16 blocks).

↗ Row 28 (WS): inc, A x 16, fasten off yarn A, turn (16 blocks).

↙ Row 29 (RS): join yarn B in last ch sp made, B x 16, turn (16 blocks).

Corner: start decreasing on WS.

↗ Row 30 (WS): dec, B x 15, turn (15 blocks).

↗ Row 31 (RS): dec, B x 14, turn (14 blocks).

↗ Row 32 (WS): dec, B x 13, fasten off yarn B, turn (13 blocks).

↙ Row 33 (RS): join yarn A in last ch sp made, A x 12, turn (12 blocks).

↙ Row 34 (WS): dec, A x 11, turn (11 blocks).

↙ Row 35 (RS): dec, A x 10, turn (10 blocks).

↗ Row 36 (WS): dec, A x 9, fasten off yarn A, turn (9 blocks).

↙ Row 37 (RS): join yarn B in last ch sp made, B x 8, turn (8 blocks).

↙ Row 38 (WS): dec, B x 7, turn (7 blocks).

↙ Row 39 (RS): dec, B x 6, turn (6 blocks).

↙ Row 40 (WS): dec, B x 5, fasten off yarn B, turn (5 blocks).

↙ Row 41 (RS): join yarn A in last ch sp made, A x 4, turn (4 blocks).

↙ Row 42 (WS): dec, A x 3, turn (3 blocks).

↙ Row 43 (RS): dec, A x 2, turn (2 blocks).

↗ Row 44 (WS): dec, A x 1, fasten off yarn A, turn (1 block).

Sew in all loose ends on WS of work.

Tassels

Using yarn C, make 10 tassels measuring 20cm (8in) long and comprising five wraps each. Using another strand of yarn C, wind ties around each tassel at the top to close the tassel. Attach to the ends of the rug, evenly spaced, using yarn C.

Sew in all loose ends on WS of work.

Cushion

This cushion is created by joining two large squares together. You could also make a throw by joining multiple squares together!

SKILL LEVEL

HOOK SIZE

5mm (US H-8)

BLOCK STITCH

3 tr block: (3 ch, 3 tr in ch sp)

CUSHION SIZE

50 x 50cm (20 x 20in)

CUSHION PAD

50 x 50cm (20 x 20in)

YARN

Cascade 220 Superwash® (DK/8-ply/ light worsted; 100g/3½oz; 200m/220yd)

	A	851 Lime – 1 ball
	B	871 White – 2 balls
	C	820 Lemon – 1 ball
	D	287 Deep Sea Coral – 1 ball
	E	1973 Seafoam Heather – 1 ball
	F	288 Green Spruce – 1 ball

ABBREVIATIONS & STITCHES

ch sp   chain space

dc   double crochet

dec   sl st in next 3 sts, sl st into 3-ch sp

inc   ch 6, 1 tr in fourth ch from hook, 1 tr in next 2 ch, sl st into ch sp of next block

RS   right side

sl st   slip stitch

st(s)   stitch(es)

tr   treble crochet

WS   wrong side

[ ]   repeat instructions between brackets number of times stated

↙/↗   direction of work

Cushion

Make 2 squares

↙ Row 1 (RS): using yarn A, 6 ch, 1 tr in fourth ch from hook and in next 2 ch (1 block).

↗ Row 2 (WS): inc, A x 1, turn (2 blocks).

↙ Row 3 (RS): inc, A x 2, turn (3 blocks).

↗ Row 4 (WS): inc, A x 3, turn (4 blocks).

↙ Row 5 (RS): inc, A x 4, turn (5 blocks).

↗ Row 6 (WS): inc, A x 5, turn (6 blocks).

↙ Row 7 (RS): inc, A x 6, fasten off yarn A, turn (7 blocks).

↗ Row 8 (WS): join yarn B in last st made, inc, B x 7, turn (8 blocks).

↙ Row 9 (RS): inc, B x 8, turn (9 blocks).

↗ Row 10 (WS): inc, B x 9, fasten off yarn B, turn (10 blocks).

↙ Row 11 (RS): join yarn C in last st made, inc, C x 10, turn (11 blocks).

↗ Row 12 (WS): inc, C x 11, turn (12 blocks).

↙ Row 13 (RS): inc, C x 12, turn (13 blocks).

↗ Row 14 (WS): inc, C x 13, turn (14 blocks).

↙ Row 15 (RS): inc, C x 14, turn (15 blocks).

↗ Row 16 (WS): inc, C x 15, fasten off yarn C, turn (16 blocks).

↙ Row 17 (RS): join yarn B in last st made, inc, B x 16, turn (17 blocks).

↗ Row 18 (WS): inc, B x 17, turn (18 blocks).

↙ Row 19 (RS): inc, B x 18, fasten off yarn B, turn (19 blocks).

↗ Row 20 (WS): join yarn D in last st made, inc, D x 19, turn (20 blocks).

↙ Row 21 (RS): inc, D x 20, turn (21 blocks).

↗ Row 22 (WS): inc, D x 21, turn (22 blocks).

↙ Row 23 (RS): inc, D x 22, turn (23 blocks).

↗ Row 24 (WS): inc, D x 23, turn (24 blocks).

↙ **Row 25 (RS):** inc, D x 24, turn (25 blocks).

↗ **Row 26 (WS):** inc, B x 25, turn (26 blocks).

↙ **Row 27 (RS):** inc, B x 26 (27 blocks).

Corner: start decreasing at both ends.

> **Important note:** Throughout the following section, if a colour is needed again along a row, carry that colour under stitches as you work your way across. This cuts out the need for bobbins, which you can use instead if you prefer.

↗ **Row 28 (WS):** dec, B x 26, fasten off yarn B, turn (26 blocks).

↙ **Row 29 (RS):** join yarn E in last ch sp made, E x 12, B x 1, F x 12, turn (25 blocks).

↗ **Row 30 (WS):** dec, F x 11, B x 2, E x 11, turn (24 blocks).

↙ **Row 31 (RS):** dec, E x 11, B x 1, F x 11, fasten off all yarn colours, turn (23 blocks).

↗ **Row 32 (WS):** join yarn B in last ch sp made, B x 9, F x 1, B x 2, E x 1, B x 9, turn (22 blocks).

↙ **Row 33 (RS):** dec, B x 8, E x 2, B x 1, F x 2, B x 8, turn (21 blocks).

↗ **Row 34 (WS):** dec, B x 8, F x 1, B x 2, E x 1, B x 8, fasten off all yarn colours, turn (20 blocks).

↙ **Row 35 (RS):** join yarn E in last ch sp made, E x 6, B x 1, E x 2, B x 1, F x 2, B x 1, F x 6, turn (19 blocks).

↗ **Row 36 (WS):** dec, F x 5, B x 2, F x 1, B x 2, E x 1, B x 2, E x 5, turn (18 blocks).

↙ **Row 37 (RS):** dec, E x 5, B x 1, E x 2, B x 1, F x 2, B x 1, F x 5, turn (17 blocks).

↗ **Row 38 (WS):** dec, F x 4, B x 2, F x 1, B x 2, E x 1, B x 2, E x 4, turn (16 blocks).

↙ **Row 39 (RS):** dec, E x 4, B x 1, E x 2, B x 1, F x 2, B x 1, F x 4, turn (15 blocks).

↗ **Row 40 (WS):** dec, F x 3, B x 2, F x 1, B x 2, E x 1, B x 2, E x 3, turn (14 blocks).

↙ **Row 41 (RS):** dec, E x 3, B x 1, E x 2, B x 1, F x 2, B x 1, F x 3, turn (13 blocks).

↗ **Row 42 (WS):** dec, F x 2, B x 2, F x 1, B x 2, E x 1, B x 2, E x 2, turn (12 blocks).

↙ **Row 43 (RS):** dec, E x 2, B x 1, E x 2, B x 1, F x 2, B x 1, F x 2, turn (11 blocks).

↗ **Row 44 (WS):** dec, F x 1, B x 2, F x 1, B x 2, E x 1, B x 2, E x 1, turn (10 blocks).

↙ **Row 45 (RS):** dec, E x 1, B x 1, E x 2, B x 1, F x 2, B x 1, F x 1, fasten off all yarn colours (9 blocks).

↗ **Row 46 (WS):** join yarn B in last ch sp made, B x 2, F x 1, B x 2, E x 1, B x 2, turn (8 blocks).

↙ **Row 47 (RS):** dec, B x 1, E x 2, B x 1, F x 2, B x 1, turn (7 blocks).

↗ **Row 48 (WS):** dec, B x 1, F x 1, B x 2, E x 1, B x 1, fasten off yarn B, turn (6 blocks).

↙ **Row 49 (RS):** pick up yarn E in last ch sp made, E x 2, B x 1, F x 2, turn (5 blocks).

↗ **Row 50 (WS):** dec, F x 1, B x 2, E x 1, turn (4 blocks).

↙ **Row 51 (RS):** dec, E x 1, B x 1, F x 1, fasten off yarn E and F, turn (3 blocks).

↗ **Row 52 (WS):** join yarn B in last ch sp made, B x 2, turn (2 blocks).

↙ **Row 53 (RS):** dec, B x 1, fasten off yarn B, turn (1 block).

Edging

↙ **Row 1 (RS):** join yarn B in any corner st, ch 1, 1 dc in same place, [ch 2, 1 dc in next gap between two blocks] twenty-six times, ch 2, [1 dc in corner st] four times omitting last dc, join with sl st to first dc made.

↙ **Row 2 (RS):** 1 ch, 3 dc in corner st, [2 dc in ch-2 sp, 1 dc in dc] twenty-four times, [2 dc in ch-2 sp] four times, join with sl st to first st made, fasten off yarn B.

Sew in all loose ends on WS of work.

Joining

With wrong sides of squares facing, sew together using any method you prefer, inserting the cushion pad when joining the last edge. Alternatively, you can crochet the squares together.

Index

Credits

For Sean.
Well, only on the condition that I get a bigger studio in the next house we buy!

A HUGE thank you to Sarah Hazell for helping with throw-making at the last minute. This book wouldn't have been finished on time without you. Thank you, you are a star!

Thanks to the ladies of The Wool Croft, Abergavenny, for your friendship and support. Especially you, Ginevra! x

Thanks to Cascade Yarns® for providing all the yarns for not just this book, but all my other books too. Such lovely yarns!

Also, thank you to the wonders of modern medicine in successfully easing RSI upsets.

Quarto would like to thank Cascade Yarns® for supplying all the yarn used in this book.

For a full list of yarns available, please visit their website: www.cascadeyarns.com

You can also find them on Instagram @cascadeyarns